SHEFFIELD BLITZ

In words, pictures and memories

By Paul License

ONE reader of The Star comments within these pages that The Blitz attacks on Sheffield changed the lives forever of the people of the city.

In just two nights of bombing, the German air force brought death and destruction on an unimaginable scale. Yet the people of Sheffield showed their true northern grit to overcome untold hardships and piece together their lives, while keeping the wheels of industry turning and helping the war effort.

I am proud that The Star has been able to publish this unique account of the Sheffield Blitz to mark the 60th anniversary of the raids.

It is unique in the way it combines words provided by Paul License, who carried out his research in old copies of The Star and associated publications, contemporary pictures from The Star's archives, which are skilfully presented by graphic designer Ann Beedham, and memories of readers of The Star.

Their generous contribution is much appreciated and I hope they are pleased with this book.

The story of the Blitz is their story.

Peter Charlton
Editor, The Star, November 2000

Contents

ⓒ Paul License and Sheffield Newspapers November 2000

Published by Sheffield Newspapers Ltd. York Street, Sheffield S1 1PU
Compiled by Paul License. Design & layout by Ann Beedham

A convoy ▶ of trams abandoned in the city centre as buildings blazed and crumbled to dust and debris

Memories from Joe Ashton

IT WAS Sheffield's proud boast that it made the weapons of war for the troops while Leeds made the WAAF's knickers. Which was why Goering never bothered bombing Leeds.

In 1860, when Prime Minister Lord Palmerston sent his gunboats up the Limpopo to sort out the natives of the British Empire, the boats would be made of Sheffield armour-plate, tough enough to stand up to any cannon. Whether he knew of the conditions the steel was made in was doubtful.

Our house in Harriet Street, off Birch Road, stood across the street from Jonas and Colver's steelworks and literally 20 yards from a drop-hammer which went crash, bang, wallop 24-hours a day. The row of outside lavs in the yard had not worked since 1899, and all of us walked round to the next

The best favour anybody did our family

street to use grandma's. There were at least a thousand cockroaches and maybe a hundred crickets (we never counted the bugs) infecting every house, breeding in the heat, soot, sparks and smoke from the forge.

Those nostalgic stories about the olden days, with a tin bath in front of the open coal fire, look good on Catherine Cookson television. In reality, it was a cruel, hard life for any steelworks family. Not necessarily grinding poverty, because, when work was plentiful, steelworkers were well paid for their hard slog and round-the-clock shifts, but an awful, often miserable existence.

In fact, the best favour anybody did our family, including two grandmas, three aunties and umpteen other extended members of the clan living within a stone's throw, was when Adolf Hitler's Luftwaffe bombed the lot of us and flattened the neighbourhood. Hitler was aiming to wipe out the centre of Britain's

armour-plate steel industry, just as our boys later demolished the Krupps' factories in the Ruhr Valley. Except that his navigators missed. On Thursday night, just before Christmas 1940, they bombed Sheffield city centre and killed 600 people in the pubs and pictures. Then, they came back on Sunday and bombed us. Another mile east and they would have obliterated the whole Don Valley, and maybe won the war. Instead, they demolished our lav and took the roof off our house and all the others in the street. Plus, they destroyed several streets, schools, shops, pubs, canal bridges, tramlines, sewers, water-pipes and gas and electricity supplies. For kids it was wonderful. Better than Bonfire Night.

A hundred yards from the steelworks was the Foundry Working Men's Club, nicknamed the 'Moulders'.

As the bombs fell, the committee quickly passed a resolution that there was no point in all the ale going to waste, especially when everybody might be dead by morning, so they let any member brave enough to stay out of the shelter take what he wanted. And the whole street did.

Fiction writers everywhere have fantasised about what folks would get up to if the end of the world was nigh. I actually saw it. My only regret is that at six-years-old, I was too young to enjoy it. I certainly do not recall anybody saying any prayers. Or starting off singing 'Abide with Me,' like they did in the war pictures. Most of the street seemed determined to go right though every single one of the seven deadly sins before the roof fell in. Including some very respectable neighbours. By some miracle, the 'Moulders', survived while all the slum houses around it were set on fire by incendiary bombs.

But not before the free booze had encouraged enough brave

◀ *Labour MP Joe Ashton has lived all his life in Sheffield.*

His childhood was spent in Attercliffe, in the industrial heartland of the city which was the prime target of the Blitz.

Here, in an extract from his autobiography Red Rose Blues, he remembers the unromantic realities of cockroaches, tin baths and smoke from the forge...

◀ *Air raid wardens were issued with whistles to supplement the sirens, half of which were knocked out in the Blitz*

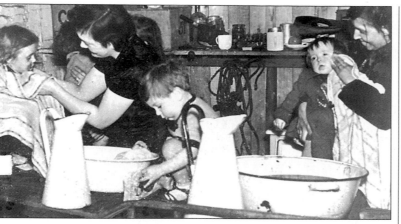

Don't forget to do behind the ears! Bath night at Anns Road, Centre, December 1940

souls to run through the flames and loot the wireless from every house. No-one cared. They were all on hire purchase, anyway.

We kids couldn't wait to get to the pictures next day to see if we would be on Pathe News doing our bit for Britain. Perhaps the King and Queen would pay us a visit like they always did to the cheering Cockneys in London's East End. Perhaps old Churchill would turn up with his Homburg hat and his two fingers up giving the V sign. He daren't, said my grandad Maloney, he barely escaped in one piece the last time he got off the train in the Sheffield depression. Attercliffe must have been one of the very few places in Dad's Army Britain where Mr Churchill got booed.

Actually, we kids should not have been involved in the bombing. When the war broke out, our school was evacuated to the fields of rural Leicestershire, with joyous mothers waving us off at Sheffield station. My mam and dad weren't half disappointed when, two weeks later, they heard a kicking on the door at ten o'clock at night and found little Joe standing on the step after hitch-hiking home with his pal, George, aged 10. We just couldn't stand the silence, the bath every night and bedtime at half past seven.

The Jerries even bombed the chip shop. Now that was a blow. With food on ration, fish and chips were one of the few pleasures available without having to produce coupons in the queue to get served. The chippies were

little goldmines. But the terrace house with our local chippy in the front room was badly damaged. There is a legend I heard years later (it had travelled to every town) that the two women running the chippy had been fading good-time girls, who bought it so that they wouldn't be compelled to work in a munitions factory. The day after the Blitz, some wag wrote on the wall in chalk, 'Thanks to Hitler, chips will be littler'.
The next day another mystery message appeared, 'Thanks to Himmler, fish will be similar'. Only to be followed the day after with, 'Thanks to Goering - gone back to whoring'.

It was marvellous, the Blitz. We never went to school for three months. Our gang kept busy trying to pull down the walls which had been left standing. Until two kids got buried, and then the council did it for us. All we had to do then was turn up at Mrs Johnson's, one of the few houses still intact, to chant the times tables for half an hour.

We lived and slept anywhere. Any relative who had a space on the floor, or under a sideboard where a kid could fit in, would do. The whole neighbourhood became an adventure playground. The council were too busy trying to run a city with no food, beer, water, street-lights or transport to bother about kids.
We just sneaked into the pictures every afternoon. We clubbed together for one kid to pay, then in the dark he would quietly

open the emergency exit for the others to creep in. We saw Boris Karloff in Frankenstein 12 times. The film was classed as 'H' for horror and restricted to over-16s, but why bother about kids being scared in a city where 630 people were killed and buried in two nights of bombing? Streetwise Artful Dodgers didn't worry about Frankenstein monsters.

We told each other real ghost stories in bombed-out cellars where dead bodies had been dug up.

To pass the time, my pal Georgie promised to take me horse-riding. There were no horses within ten miles of Attercliffe, except the one which pulled the Co-op milkman's cart, so he simply borrowed that.

And the milk tokens too. George kept the horse for a week on the canal bank, and only got found out when he took it to his auntie's to show her how he could ride bareback better than Geronimo. The only problem was that he didn't notice the clothes-line across the yard, and when the horse went under it George got garrotted. Fortunately for Georgie, the magistrate was a kindly Old Labour JP. He was nicknamed as 'The Judge', because he always carried an unrolled umbrella when he went round collecting insurance in his starched 'Sick and Divide' wing-collar. The Judge said it was obvious that the lad loved horses, and the animal had been well-fed and had no doubt enjoyed the rest. What's more, as the Co-op had got all its milk tokens back, he would simply report the matter to the boy's headmaster so that he could take the necessary steps. George said nowt about the school being bombed and the teachers all away, but just touched his forelock and said, 'Thank you, Mester Judge,' and as counselling, or social worker's reports, hadn't even been invented, that was that.

Joe Ashton

*Taken from Joe's autobiography, **Red Rose Blues**, published by Macmillan.*

1 The price of war

◀ *This is one of the most famous scenes from the Sheffield Blitz, showing a stricken tram sillhouetted against a blazing building*

One of these genuine raids...

In two nights of bombing, the Luftwaffe's planes claimed the lives of more than 668 civilians and 25 servicemen.

Another 92 people were reported missing. A further 1,586 people were injured and 40,000 made homeless. Among those who perished were 13 ARP wardens, who died on duty. Several others were injured.

A total of 3,000 homes were demolished, another 3,000 badly damaged and 72,000 suffered some damage.

Eight gasholders were knocked out and gas supplies widely disrupted. The bombs had fractured 206 water mains and broken 90 sewers. A total of 50 electricity sub stations were out of action. On the roads 22 buses were destroyed or seriously

IN Sheffield, the alert was sounded 130 times during the war. Almost all of them were false alarms, triggered by enemy aircraft flying over the region on their way to other targets. But on 16 occasions, the alarms were genuine.
One of these genuine alarms sounded at 7pm on Thursday, December 12, 1940.
That was the night the Blitz came to Sheffield...

damaged and 857 street lamps destroyed or seriously damaged. More than 3,000 telephone lines were damaged and more than 1,200 shops and business premises destroyed, with a further 2,255 so badly damaged they were unusable.

TRAM cars took a battering in the Blitz. When the chaos was sorted out, 31 cars were seriously damaged, 11 of them burnt out, and 14 so badly wrecked that they had to be written-off. Another 29 cars needed a week's repair work and 88 had minor damage, mostly broken windows. Before a limited service could be started again, the wrecked and damaged trams had to be carted away and miles of overhead lines repaired after breaks were reported in 30 different places. New tram poles were also needed in parts of the city, especially on The Moor. Using components from some of the damaged vehicles, 14 'new trams' were built at Queens Road works as replacements, 14 trams were bought from Newcastle and ten more from Bradford.

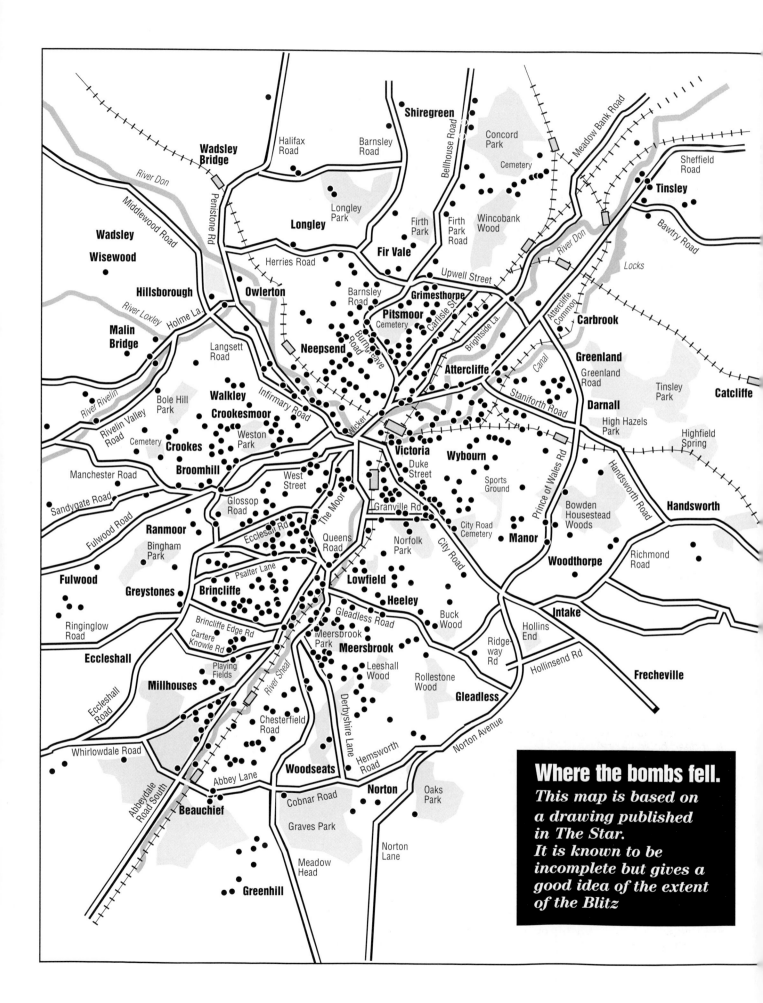

Where the bombs fell.

*This map is based on a drawing published in The Star.
It is known to be incomplete but gives a good idea of the extent of the Blitz*

Ted Street remembers

◀ *Ted Street in his younger days*

THE Thursday night Blitz had begun before I was due to start work on nights at Kayser Ellison steelworks, in Darnall. I remember the shrapnel falling as I walked to work…luckily none hit me! Some of my mates also turned up but no work was done, everything was shut down because of the raid.

As usual, whenever a raid was on I made my way to a small fire-spotter's shelter which was on a roof on a high bank at the back of the factory. I watched the city being bombed and set on fire, the anti-aircraft guns firing and saw two German planes in the searchlight which followed them across the skies. The shells from the guns seemed to be exploding not at all close to the planes (we now know that the aircraft flew beyond the range of the guns.)

When my shift was over at 6am, myself and a couple of mates decided to walk up town to see the damage. When we got to the Wicker Arches, it was havoc. We had to walk under the main arch as the side ones, which had been made into air raid shelters, were out of bounds. Someone said that dead bodies were in there. I remember a hole through the roof of the main arch. Among the wrecked tramcars in the Wicker was one which was completely in two and overhead wires all around. I remember there was a pub on fire near the top of Dixon Lane, in Haymarket. The fire crews had cordoned it off and I remember a chap who must have just come out of an air raid shelter trying to push his way past a fireman to get into the building. He said he was the landlord and wanted to get inside to get the money. A fireman told him there was no way he would allow him into the blazing building.

A little further on we reached Fitzalan Square where the Marples had suffered a direct hit. There were men in khaki uniforms amid the rubble. We and other men offered to help but they wouldn't allow anyone to so do. The C&A and Walsh's stores were very badly damaged and still on fire and High Street was blocked off so we made our way up Norfolk Street which was covered in debris, mud, water…a real mess. We got to the top of High Street via Chapel Walk and there was a WVS van with ladies giving people cups of tea. While enjoying a cup of tea, there was a loud band which we guessed was an unexploded bomb going off. It was then we decided to go home. Sheffield had suffered badly but the steelworks had more or less escaped. Of course the Sunday Blitz was different.

On that night, I travelled on a tramcar up Prince of Wales Road to Manor Top and walked to the home of a workmate, Fred White, on Arbourthorne Estate. Soon after I arrived, sirens sounded and we guessed it would be another big raid and this time at the steelworks. We stood on the porch looking out and could see the sky light up.

The next morning, Fred and I set off to walk to work but first I called to see if my folk were all right. Along the way, we saw houses in Prince of Wales Road and Ravencarr Road which had been hit. It looked worse as we got to Darnall, looking up Ribston Road where a chip shop was flattened and still burning. Across the road three or four houses were also demolished. My home was about 70 yards away. It was with my heart in my mouth that I approached home. Luckily it was still standing but the windows were broken and the roof damaged. My folk were OK except for my grandfather. He had undergone surgery a couple of days before and he had been in bed in the living room when the ceiling fell in on him. He took a turn for the worse and had to go back into hospital, which I believe was the Firvale workhouse which had been converted to make room for people needing to be in hospital. A short time after, he died.

Fred and I eventually got to work to find the roof badly damaged even though there had been no direct hit. All around, Whixlcy Road, Bridport Road, Helenor Street, the Brown Bailey steelworks (where the stadium now stands) had all suffered direct hits. I cannot remember how the rest of the steelworks were affected but I know all were very soon back to near full production. Sheffield took a hell of a beating during the two nights of the Blitz and had numerous lesser raids. It did its share during the war and Sheffielders should be proud. I am! ❞

▼ *Ted as he is today*

Ted Street

who was a 17 year old steelworker at the time of the Blitz

Mrs Oden remembers

❝ WHEN my family came to Sheffield, we rented a six-bedroomed house at 13, Devonshire Road, Totley Rise for £80 a year. My father got it cheap because nobody wanted to rent a house numbered 13 during the war! My father was in Sheffield throughout the Blitz and told the story of a millionaire who built an air raid shelter in his garden. The walls and roof were made of 6-feet-thick concrete and it was considered indestructible. A bomb came straight down through the house to the cellar and its blast came up through the earth floor of the shelter, killing everybody. No one can avoid fate. ❞

Mrs H A Oden

This is ▶ Sheffield's best kept secret of the war. The 15 ton drop hammer at Vickers works was the only one in the country making the Rolls Royce crankshafts which kept our fleet of Spitfires and Hurricanes in the air during the Battle of Britain and beyond. The Germans hit the factory, but missed the hammer…and the war effort continued

6

2 Target: Industry

◀ *Production in the steelworks went on throughout the war and even continued during many air raids. A decision was taken to stop work only when the foundries' own rooftop spotters reported the presence of enemy aircraft overhead. (They were trained to tell the difference between friend and foe!)*

THE Germans knew that Sheffield was the key to Britain's resistance. The city's steel works turned out the raw materials and munitions which kept our forces armed and dangerous. The steel works and foundries were the principal target for the raiders when they came in their hundreds on December 12 and 15. But though they caused some damage to the industrial premises, a mighty pulse beat throughout the attacks and continued afterwards to produce one of the most vital components for the whole war effort.

At the English Steel Corporation's Vickers works in the east end, was to be found a 15 ton drop hammer, housed in a 200 ton mounting, whose regular beats could be heard for miles around. If the bombers had struck here, in a half square mile of grime and toil, they would

Beating out the vital engine parts...

have done irreparable damage to the war effort. For the hammer was the only one in the land capable of turning out Rolls Royce Merlin crankshafts for the Spitfire and Hurricane aircraft which won the Battle of Britain. Manned by 16 men working in two shifts, the hammer produced 168 stampings a day, one of the three operations necessary in the creation of a fighter plane crankshaft. And for another 18 months, the drop hammer remained the only one of its kind in the country, steadily rising and

falling on the raw metal and beating out the vital engine parts which helped turn the tide of war. It is almost certain that if German intelligence had learned this nugget of information, the raids would have continued until the hammer was silenced. As it was, the German high command knew that Sheffield was the centre for turning out armour plate and other vital materials for the British forces.

▼ *Bomb damage at the works of George Wostenholm and Son Ltd., in Wellington Street*

Blitz ▶ *damage at W T Flather Ltd. Soldiers help with the clear up*

Their intention on the two nights that they launched intense bombing raids on Sheffield was no doubt to knock out and damage as many of the steelworks as possible while at the same time terrorising the people who worked in them.

The ESC works would have been on the German target list, along with other steelworks producing armour plate. The ESC plant also turned out springs and components for tanks, side and deck armour for warships, bomb casings and the forgings for half

of the country's 17 pounder anti-tank guns. The workforce were proud of their record in responding to rush jobs. When the Allies were later to prepare for the Normandy Landings the men and women of ESC produced armour plate for the landing crafts.

This came in eighteen 1,150 ton sets, each made up of 59 individual plates.

And they also came to the rescue when HMS Valiant was hit by a mine.

▼*IT was not only the steelworks which were bombed by the Germans, who are renowned to be one of Europe's biggest beer drinking nations.*

The letter of appreciation reproduced here belongs to Mrs Sylvia Houghton, who emigrated to Vancouver, Canada, in 1951, whose father Mr Whiley received a £5 reward for his efforts.

It was forwarded by Mrs M Thorpe, of Sheffield.

Edith Thorpe remembers

" *I CAN well remember the Blitz. I was living in Queens Road and saw the devastation of trams all burnt out and everything on fire. I was pregnant at the time and had to go and take shelter in our cellar. I really thought I should have a miscarriage, I was frightened to death. On top of all that, December 12 was my birthday! I had made a cake for myself, but what with the bombing and the shattering of windows, I never got to eat it and it ended up in bits. We had no water, no lights, I really thought this was it! Thankfully, I survived ...... and had a lovely daughter in March!*

Edith Thorpe
a birthday and the Blitz "

Old Albion Brewery Ltd

TELEPHONE: SHEFFIELD 26648
TELEGRAMS: ALBION SHEFFIELD

ECCLESALL ROAD,
SHEFFIELD, 11.

December 16th 1940

Dear Whiley

It is difficult to show my full appreciation of your valuable efforts in saveing the Brewery premises from serious damage during the Air raid on Thursday night 12th inst but please accept my grateful thanks for all you have done.

Yours sincerely

Wm H. Allen

The warship's propeller was buckled and the teams at ESC had another rush job on their hands, working round the clock to make the parts and send them off to their destination. Other famous names from the city's great industrial era also played their part. The Steel, Peech and Tozer Ickles Works directed half of its wartime work towards forging parts for guns. These could be anything from a 2 pounder anti-tank weapon to a 6 inch naval gun. In 1942, the workforce brought honour on themselves when it was remarked that their gun components output made up the largest delivered by a single forging firm in the UK. continued on P11

This picture, of the RAF's 10 ▶ ton bombs in manufacture, carried the following caption when printed by The Star: "Great secrecy was observed during production of this picture. Much of the work was done by the English Steel Corporation, Sheffield. The illustration was taken at a Ministry of Supply filling factory where holes had to be dug in the floor to enable the workers to operate. Extreme accuracy of manufacture was demanded for the production of our latest giant bombs." Bombs like these sank the German battleship Tirpitz

◀ *A Matilda tank crashes through a brick barrier at a Rotherham factory during a demonstration for staff*

Arnold ▶ *Laver's woodyard in Bramall Lane. So fierce were the flames and intense the heat that it was ruefully reported that not a scrap of useful wood survived*

A table in a ▶ *factory is covered with flowers and workers bow their heads in tribute to a girl colleague killed by a bomb. Sadly this scene would have been acted out many times over after the Blitz*

The company produced almost 4 million tons of steel ingots, nearly 3 million tons of part-finished steel with much of it going to Templeborough's bar and strip mills where it was turned into 270,000 tons of shell steel bars. Another firm, Edgar Allen and Co, increased its stainless steel output by a staggering 700 per cent in the first year of the war. Warships, aircraft and submarines accounted for the bulk of this raw material.

The plant also turned out enough metal for 1,115,600 helmets for the forces and enough bullet core sheets to make 28,114,016 bullets. Meanwhile, the trackwork department kept the nation's railways moving and, simultaneously, was kept busy drilling, machining and tapping tank plates as well as grinding out almost a million aircraft parts.

◀ *Newspaper advertisement encouraging people to invest in defence bonds*

The nation's tank regiments also owed a huge debt of gratitude to the steelworkers, who produced 872 Matilda tank turrets, another 515 for Churchill tanks and a further 116,743 tank components. It was little surprise, therefore, that the Luftwaffe should be told sooner rather than later to target Sheffield.

One recollection of the effect of the bombs on the city comes from Mr CB Glover, of Chapeltown. He said: "After the war I was an apprentice electrician at Brown Bayleys, who put on a show for their staff showing photographs of things that happened during the Blitz.

"One thing I remember was a five-ton ingot which, when No 1 Mill was hit by three high explosive bombs, was blown out of Brown Bayleys, across the common and was found in Hadfield's steelworks in Newhall Road. It just looked as if someone had pulled handsfull of metal out of it!"

So important was the role of the east end industries to the nation's war effort that a special Sheffield and District Production Defence Committee was set up to advise firms on how to keep working despite the air raids. Production had been affected badly by false alarms, when planes overflew the region. As a result it was decided to carry on working in Sheffield's factories and steelworks even during air raids.

Workers would only halt production when their own rooftop spotters reported that there were enemy planes in the area.

Another decision taken, to help keep the steelworks in production, was for scrap railings to be requisitioned.

Teams foraged the country and turned in 350,000 tons of scrap, enough to make 23,333 tanks.

Jack Morley remembers

Jack ▶ Morley in 1939

Mr Morley ▲ was one of the first messenger lads, aged 16 in 1939. He transferred to the newly-formed LDV (Home Guard) when it was formed following Dunkirk in 1940 and in June 1941, joined the RAF and served as wireless operator/AG

" I set out for work on the afternoon shift on that fateful Thursday in December 1940, little realising the events which were to unfold later that evening, and the profound effect they would have on my life.

Arriving at work, taking over from the morning shift, we carried on throughout the afternoon until, by the time we had poured out our penultimate heat, and recharged the furnaces, there was the sound of air raid sirens. The sound of gunfire and exploding bombs seemed all around. As the metal became hot enough to pour, there was the terrific bang of a nearby bomb and the shop filled with dust as the whole roof was dislodged, then dropped back again.

My first instinct was to dash outside, but our foreman Albert said that before leaving, as we were all safe, we should continue to teem the metal, then drop the fires and clear the moulds. This we did. After completing the teeming, some of the shift tidied up the furnace areas, while the rest of us went down to the cellars, withdrawing the bars beneath the furnaces, to allow the burning cokes to drop into the safe space below. Once this was done, we moved along the line of moulds, knocking out wedges which held the iron rings in place, to hold the moulds in position, then knocking down the front of each mould, and with tongs removing the hot ingots and stacking them. Then, a quick wash, and home, not knowing what the night still had in store.

By the time we left the premises, the raid had been in progress for a couple of hours, and our position, the bottom end of Rockingham Street, in the centre of town, was a most precarious one. We lived at various districts spread over the city, and all would have to walk. My own companions for the journey were a couple of lads of my own age, Walt and Lawrence, both of whom lived in Manor and Wybourn areas. But once outside Lawrence ran off in a different direction to us two. We had decided that as most fires seemed to be towards The Moor, we would try to skirt around them, up towards Division Street for a start, but were soon disillusioned, as there was a bombed out fire tender across our path and burning. Retracing our steps, we could see huge fires in the direction of the Central Picture Palace, and decided to try Button Lane, towards Moorhead.

Here, we were met by burning buildings at both sides of the lane, a scene reminiscent of the picture, "All Quiet On The Western Front," and Ypres. But there was a seemingly clear path up the centre. Full of forebodings now, Walt and I ran as fast as we could, until we reached the comparative safety of Moorhead. No fires here but, as we studied the inferno lower down the Moor, my companion noticed parachutes coming down. In that instant, a fast moving policeman passed us, shouting as he went: "Run you fools, they're landmines."

◄ *A tram which had been bound for Intake split in two in the Wicker. This was the scene on December 13, the day after the first Blitz on the city. Notice the bomb crater filling with water alongside the tram. Damaged water mains caused a new menace for the people of Sheffield in the days after the Blitz - how to get clean water*

Needing no second bidding, we ran towards Union Street, past the said bobby, and dived beneath a fire tender which had fallen into the bomb crater outside the Empire Theatre, he followed seconds later. After catching our breath, we continued our traumatic journey home. Bombs fell all around as we tried to get home, an unreal atmosphere, and a most frightening passage through the heart of our city. First towards Fargate, retracing our steps, down Norfolk Street, along Change Alley, down Angel Street.

At this point, Walt left me, and made his way towards the bottom of High Street, where there was great activity, the scene of the bombed Marples Hotel. I went down Angel Street, past the burning Cockayne's store which looked as if a plane had crashed on

it. A not-very-pleasant sight here, as what looked like a pair of gloved hands, clutched a piece of hosepipe, as if someone fighting the fire had tragically been blown to bits. Continuing towards Castle Street, I turned down Water Lane, past the back entrance of the old Town Hall, and the cells below the court house. Down to Bridge Street, past the brewery entrance and the Lady's Bridge Hotel, then towards the Wicker. Here, on the bridge, a chap said to me, "Give me a lift with this, and help me throw it into the river." The object was some sort of incendiary bomb. Years later, this chap became my brother-in-law, but it was only some time later when I heard him recounting the experience, that we both realised the coincidence of our first meeting,

Tom Leigh and I. My journey continued along the Wicker, negotiating glass and rubble all around. Past the burning bottom half of a tram-car, opposite the end of Stanley Street, with the other half also burning, but leaning up against the front of Bentley's car showroom where it had been thrown. Just as I arrived at the pedestrian part of the Wicker Arches, which had been walled in at each end, for use as a shelter, the all clear sounded. As I went to enter, a policeman told me that I could not proceed, as there was nothing left at the other side, to which I replied that as my home was through there, he was not going to stop me from finding out for myself what had happened to my brothers and sister, parents, grandad and uncles, as we all lived together. My lasting

memory of that shelter, as I passed through, though I have never seen any reference to it, was that people were standing up dead against the wall, with mouths wide open, as if the blast from the bomb which hit the main arch, alongside them, had drawn their life breath from their bodies. Onward now, up a deserted Spital Hill, a strange silence now taking the place of the gunfire, and explosions. Passing the shops, all with shattered windows then, turning up Bramber Street, my heart sinking, passing the many bomb damaged houses with broken windows, and still not a person in sight. Not daring to think what may be found, I turned into our entry to hear mum say: "Thank God, he's here."

J Morley
Who worked through the raid

Fred ▲ Peacock today. At the time of the Blitz he worked as a draughtsman for James Neill & Co.

"THURSDAY was early closing day for the shops and evening school at Leopold Street for me. The class was soon alerted to the raid at 7pm and we were directed to the cellars, packing our drawing boards and instruments on the way down. This was a repeat of the previous Thursday at exactly the same time and for some reason rather than join my mates at cards again I simply wanted to watch. Then I suddenly felt the need to catch the tram home. The Town Hall square was desolate with not a soul in site, just a clear sky with signs of smoke drifting from somewhere. A tram appeared. Lucky for me it was to Ecclesall. As it stopped and I saw it had no passengers, I became scared somewhat. Having to sit in front of glass windows I promptly propped my drawing board behind me. The conductor had an air of uncertainty about him and I held out a penny as the tram moved hastily

down The Moor. I cast my eyes upward - Glory, the heavens had opened! All the tops of the shops were on fire, lighting up the sky and soon we came to a standstill. A tram was in flames in front, blocking the junction to Ecclesall. Being a draughtsman, I loved creation, but not this kind. Slates were dropping from the roofs and I had the presence of mind to hold my board above my head as they landed with a clatter. I quickly decided my workplace was my destination and treaded warily towards Napier Street arriving at James Neill & Co inside the top gates at Summeffield Street to find the new toolroom on fire and a fireman directing his hose, fed from the River Porter. Not being used to all this sudden activity, I stood still, my drawing board by my side, wondering what on earth to do when I felt a tap on my shoulder. "Who are you?" It was a tall man with a trilby, who I recognised.

"Peacock, sir, drawing office" I said. And came the reply: "Frederick Neill, here." I couldn't believe my eyes. The chairman himself, excusing himself for the delay after being stuck in a bomb crater up Cemetery Road. He was concerned at the toolroom fire and said: "Follow me," as a cluster of bombs fell, yet he showed no emotion, having been a colonel in the 1914 War.

"We must find the works keyboard, it's missing," he said.

We located it with the night control caretaker who was badly burned opening the doors for the firemen. I then ventured to the drawing office to phone mum. She immediately said "Manchester is in for it tonight."

"No, it's us," and the telephone line went blank. I then recalled 'iron' rations were stored at the start of the War and we often wondered what kind they were. Surely, this was a good excuse to

sample them and took a good bite in the dark and nearly choked - they were certainly past their sell-by date. A workman was seen. "Are you all right?" I called. He replied "Those magnet men did a good job earlier on." "What was that?"

"Kicking live incendiaries off the main roof and office block."

"Take shelter, mate, things are getting hot," I said.

Having deposited my drawing board I took a walk rather gingerly to Renton Street Works to find the petrol station flattened and smouldering. This is it, I thought. Where's the nearest shelter? I remembered access to the magnet cellar by a grating in the path opposite and scrambled down to find an emergency light on and settled down to read my homework again and was glad of the chance to relax when up went the grate and a voice balled out "Come out anyone down there. The razor works above are on fire and you'll be flooded out soon," I joined a dozen men in single file led by a fireman to the cellars of the Twist Drill Company nearby.

Fred in 1942 ▶ (fourth from left) with other members of the drawing office

14

We were met by a host of men and women from the night shift, singing away. How well I remember the song, too. 'South of the border down Mexico way - That's where I fell in love when "stars" above came out to play." Some stars, I thought, more like bombs as they hurtled down 5 4 3 2 1 getting louder, then softer, thank God. Occasionally, the floor shuddered as we all laid on the stone floor thankful, no doubt, that we were relatively safe and gently singing the night away.

I can only remember the "All Clear" after that, at 7am, having dozed off to sleep, apparently like many others. As I walked along Summerfield Street I waved to a vigilant fireman who had been quenching the flames all night. And the building was just a puff of smoke. But he'd saved a block of property adjoining, in spite of a couple of houses in a terrace block opposite the river being flattened. There was a shelter nearby so the occupants could have been saved. As I entered Ecclesall Road I stood aghast to see windows blown out and bed-room linen and a mattress hanging from the tram wires. My worst fear of the Blitz night, I suppose, was stepping on to that tramcar.

It should have been the least worry, but in hindsight it prepared me for things to come. Each 'episode' seemed to guide me to final safety... **99**

Fred Peacock
who met the boss as the works burned

Soldiers from the regular army joined the thousands of volunteers who helped clear debris after the Blitz. Here they work on Walker and Hall's ◄ *building*

▼*This was a one man pill-box shelter at Blackburn Meadows Power Station for key staff. The bulk of the workforce headed for underground shelters*

Putting their best feet forward is a squad of women Home Guard troops parading through Sheffield on a rainy afternoon. Their sergeant in front wears the care-worn look of a man out-numbered

3 Preparing for war

It didn't take a military genius to realise that Sheffield was in Hitler's firing line. With such vital industry on its doorstep, and a population with the kind of knowledge to keep that industry turning which only comes from generations of experience, it was only a matter of time before the Luftwaffe planes would appear overhead. Luckily the time it took for the Germans to turn their attentions to Sheffield, more than a year, was enough for the city to go a long way to preparing for war.

One of the first, and most obvious, moves was to introduce a black out. This was a qualified success. When the lights went out and people observed the regulations, there was a hazard introduced into the lives of the people of Sheffield, who were not used to going about their way in total darkness. In the first month of 1940, 16 people died on the roads in Sheffield, 14 of them in the blackout.

As a consequence, the next month a modified blackout was introduced. Instead of the total darkness which was taking some getting used to, the street lights came back...but on a much reduced basis. The Starlight System involved hooding and dimming the lights so they

A constant patrol as the bombs rained down...

could not be seen from the air. It was first introduced in the city centre and then extended to other areas. The alarming number of night time accidents reduced almost immediately. But accidents still did happen and in September the Sheffield Home Safety Committee said it was worried about the number of accidents involving seven to 13 year olds and asked for a blackout curfew on all school age children. Meanwhile, a civilian army was being mobilised to help with the defence of Sheffield. There

◀ A rattling good idea! This ARP warden sounds a rattle to announce the discovery of gas during a wartime exercise in the south of Sheffield. "This method," reported The Star at the time, "may seem rather reminiscent of the old night watchmen who preceded the establishment of police but it proves quite effective in practice."

was no disguising the grim task these trained but untried teams faced. Under Town Clerk Basil Gibson the newly formed ARP committee made a decision which was not made public at the time. But it was grimly realistic: an order was placed for 300 coffins, at 25 shillings each, 500 hessian bags costing £21, and an unpublished number of canvas shrouds at two shillings and sixpence each.

More preparations included the requisitioning of basements and the like which were suitable to be used as shelters.

◀ Searchlights, protected by a turf wall, picked out the raiders giving ack-ack crews chance to defend the city

Schools and public buildings were also to be used as shelters and rest and sleeping centres should the people of Sheffield be made homeless.

In hospitals, patients fit enough were discharged. Others were transferred from the Royal Hospital, City General Hospital, Jessop Hospital, Royal Infirmary and Children's Hospital to what were believed to be safer buildings, mainly Nether Edge Hospital. This was to prove to be an unforeseeable but fateful mistake.

Out on Strines and Burbage Moors and in Eckington Woods, fake cities were built of oil tanks filled with oil, shavings and tin-foil to be set alight and act as decoys and the anti-aircraft and searchlight positions began to appear around the city. Meanwhile, thousands were enrolling into the Wardens' service, casualty services, Auxiliary Fire Service, Women's Voluntary Service and other organisations, such as nursing, driving, manning field kitchens, rescue, ambulance services and the Home Guard. The Special Constabulary was expanded and the City Engineer's Department given the job of ensuring there were enough civilian shelters, as well as being trained to handle rescue and decontamination work.

The barrage balloon units, part of the Auxiliary Air Force, were

Receiving ▶ you loud and clear! An NFS radio operator takes down a message from one of their radio-equipped tenders

among the first organisations to put out a call for volunteers. The balloons were to be raised above the city, forcing the bombers to fly higher than their pilots would like and make their bomb aimers' job more difficult. In Sheffield, more than 1,000 men volunteered and were responsible on the first night of the Blitz for launching 72 balloons.

Forty seven of them were damaged by enemy action or shell splinters. All were back in action within 12 hours of the all-clear being sounded. On another occasion, one particularly frosty night caused 40 balloons to come down when they became frost-bound.

The Sheffield WVS was formed in 1939, its HQ in Church Street. Hospital Supply Depots soon followed in Fulwood Road and Tapton Court. Volunteers were kept busy there making bandages and hospital clothing. By the end of December, there were 1,600 WVS members in the city.

The Air Raid Patrol crews were to prove their bravery over and again through the war years, but possibly never more clearly than when the bombers came to blitz their city. They kept up a constant patrol as the bombs rained down, offering advice and giving out stern warnings where needed. In the Blitz, many wardens lost their lives or were injured. Though there was a great sense of cameraderie and purpose of duty among the ARP, life did not go well all the time for them. A month before the Blitz on Sheffield, a big recruitment campaign was abandoned as a failure. A rally involving 200 ARP staff found only four volunteers. A rattled Chief Warden, Capt Clement Roberts said that, especially in the north and east of the city, people were not prepared to join the ARP. There would be no more campaigns, he said: "If certain districts are short of wardens it is entirely their own fault and they must accept the responsibility."

◀ The Blitz was one of the best classrooms for the trained but untested volunteers who formed home defences. After the Blitz, the training went on. In March, 1941, The Star reported: "Realistic first aid exercises were carried out by the Beighton and Frecheville first aid posts at Beighton.

Picture shows 'casualties' being treated at the Beighton post. While over 30 were being treated at one time, a large number of additional 'cases' were drafted in, in an endeavour to create chaos. They were unsuccessful. The test was a complete success"

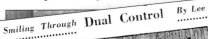

Smiling Through **Dual Control** By Lee

"Yes, my Willie's out every night now watching for fires, and I'm out every night, too . . . watching him."

◀ A stirrup pump, a hose and a job which had to be done. Volunteers practice a routine which all too soon would become a vital necessity. This picture, from The Star's archive, is marked 'Not submitted for censor'

Practice ▶ makes perfect. Here an ARP warden is busy in a gas exercise in Rygate and Evelyn Roads

In the first months of the war, the ARP had been disrupted as a row broke out over plans to reorganise them. There was a mass resignation by 24 officers in the first aid and mobile sections and several volunteer control officers at HQ also quit. The reorganisation involved putting a doctor in charge of each first aid post and dispensing with the services of the divisional officers who had previously been in charge of the posts. The reorganisation went ahead as planned, but the row rumbled on for several weeks.

The regular fire service was boosted as early as 1938 by an auxiliary service. And they were to need it when Sheffield was turned into a cauldron of fire on December 12. Under its new powers, the service opened a new station on the Manor Estate

and by the outbreak of the war there were 20 fire stations, with 500 full time and 400 part time fire crew members.

Another team who gave up their time to 'do their bit' were members of the Local Defence Force. These were better known as the Home Guard who were formed after Anthony Eden announced the news on a radio broadcast on May 14.
The first Sheffield men to volunteer turned up at local police stations even before Mr Eden had finished his broadcast and by

8pm the next day, 1,849 men had come forward in Sheffield and 500 in Rotherham. Two weeks later Col FA Neill, CO of the Sheffield LDF was able to announce that response had exceeded all expectations with thousands, many of them old soldiers, registered.
"And they are a fine type," boasted the colonel.

Despite today's image of a poorly organised, incompletely armed and over-the-hill force, the real Dad's Army played a key role in wartime operations.

They may be ▶ subject of a comedy TV programme now, but the Home Guard were vital during the war. This team of Home Guardsmen manned an anti-aircraft emplacement and have just received certificates of merit from the northern command for their role during the Blitz. They are BSM Dawson, CSM Saltfleet, Colour Sgt Nutbrown and Sgt RJ Haigh.

◀ Ready for action - members of the Auxiliary Fire Service outside the fire station in Chapel Street, Woodhouse. The fire engine is an old roadster car with a ladder strapped to the roof and a hose fastened to the mudguard on the other side of the vehicle

◀ The war was a great time for liberating women form their traditional roles in the home. These women are members of the National Fire Service setting off on a tender for a trial

Members of ▶
the National
Fire Service
pose proudly
for the
cameras.

◀ *WVS members busy making brushes for use in the works around Sheffield*

◀ *Meals on wheels. This WVS canteen was actually found on the site of the old Sun Inn, near Doncaster and offered refreshments to convoys travelling along the Great North Road. Seen are members of the Sprotborough WVS*

W.V.S. CANTEEN

Everything stops for tea. The WVS serve up refreshing cuppas in St Mary's Road to bewildered men and women who were trying to salvage something from their blitzed homes. Notice the cast iron fireplaces dangling from the walls of what would once have been bedrooms

Another clear sign of Britain preparing for the worst was the sight of children being evacuated. But in Sheffield, only 15 per cent of the city's children were moved in the final days of peace in 1939. They were put on a convoy of trains heading for places as distant as Newark, Loughborough and Melton Mowbray. The take up of the offer of evacuation was slow with the trains moving out only partially full.

And a second evacuation exercise later in the year was similarly poorly supported. By the end of the year, all but 2,000 of the evacuated children were back in Sheffield.

Those WVS ladies got everywhere! Here they hand out pies to farm workers

One person who was evacuated in the opposite direction, was Mr CB Glover, of Chapeltown. He was living in Rayleigh, Essex at the outbreak of war and, with his school pals, was treated to the sight of dog fights overhead as he made his way home after lessons.

He recalled: "The Luftwaffe were over us well before the sirens sounded. We used to watch the dog fights and were ushered home by wardens."

He was moved from this perilous place to somewhere which his parents thought would be safer: "Many of my friends were being evacuated to New Zealand, Canada and Australia. My father having joined up, it was decided I should be evacuated to Sheffield where my grandparents lived. And we ran slap bang into the Thursday night Sheffield Blitz!"

Another evacuee who found she had moved to somewhere equally as dangerous as her first home was Florence Shaw. She had lived in Deal in Kent but, when France was overrun, moved with her five year old son to Sheffield to stay with her mother. That meant she was in Sheffield for the night of the Blitz, and recalled: "Throughout the night I wondered what was happening and thought in some way that I had prepared myself for what I would see next morning. But it was far worse than I had ever dreamed. The whole of the city was a shocking sight. There were fires still burning everywhere and flames still licking out of shop windows." She soon moved back to Deal: "It was only about 20 miles from the German guns but somehow it seemed safer and, although I loved Sheffield as I love my own life, I just wanted to get away from it."

Vi Cartledge remembers

"I WAS on duty at Carbrook School, a volunteer, and as soon as the sirens went we were rushed to the ambulance. We picked up two policemen who had had a buzz bomb explode in their faces. My driver had to drive with the off-side wheels on the pavement. I was trying to hold down two poor blokes, but we landed on the floor. When we arrived at the City General Hospital there were no lights anywhere and we had just passed through the gates when a bomb dropped. I had to hold a lantern to help the doctors, then had to help to take the poor chaps across the grounds, holding bowls over their faces to shield them from shrapnel and falling debris.

On the Sunday night, my driver and I had to cope with a fire in the ambulance roof. I am 76 years old now but never for one moment do I regret my voluntary work."

Vi Cartledge
ambulance crew member

◀ *Smiles all round as an all-women ARP team get to work cleaning one of their fleet of ambulances. The ARP Ambulance Service was invaluable during the Blitz nights*

◀ *Remember saving milk bottle tops? In the war, this charitable task had a more serious side with the collected metal used for the war effort. The boy scouts played a key role in the work. It was just one of the National Service jobs the movement took on*

Kenneth Pheasey remembers

Kenneth ▶
Pheasey
in his
fireman's
uniform
in 1940

"

AFTER helping to fight fires on The Moor, December 12 and days after, I had 24 hours' rest, then it started all over again on the Sunday night. This is where the fun started. The fire crew I was with was led by Bill Turns (AFS and NFS). We were sent to a fire at Laver's wood yard in Bramall Lane. Trams were burning nearby when we all saw what we thought was a parachute bomb coming down near the ground. We all ran like hell. Being the smallest, I was last but I looked back and started laughing. It was only a barrage balloon that had broken loose, so I shouted: "Come back you fools.

"

Kenneth ▶
today

Kenneth Pheasey
(ex-fireman 1068 joined in 1938, AFS, NFS)

Public ▶
notice
urging
people to be
prepared for
action

sop Rd.). Private lessons daily from 10 a

L.   ...TON SALON, Rotherha
      Acc... ...ing every Sat., Tu
      Fri. ... Thurs. ... Sat. Afternoon,

PUBLIC NOTICES

STEVE'S SHOOTING SALOON
18, CAMBRIDGE STREET.

The R.A.F. dropped 20,000 fire bomb
on Bremen!
Smuts says we shall be invaded!!
You MUST be prepared!   Learn to sho
at Steve's.
...en daily, including Sunday, till black-ou

Newspaper ▶
ad for
Fennings
ointment,
good for
those
parading
feet!

YOU CAN HELP MAKE ME A PLANE!

Every man and woman of Great Britain is needed to win this war. *Ask yourself* one question—"Am I doing all I can to bring victory nearer?"

Employers in the Munitions Industries must prepare to take on more and more recruits—particularly women. More and more new recruits must be trained in the works.

Employers engaged on work not vital to the war effort must make it easy for their workpeople to volunteer for the Munitions Army.

And you who have never thought of doing factory work . . . now is the time to begin! Experience does not matter—you can be trained. Enquire at the nearest Local Office of the Ministry of Labour and National Service (but do not leave your present job until you are advised to do so). If you cannot possibly join the Munitions Army, at least see that you encourage those who do. Open your door and billet them when they come to work nearby. Respect them as the fighters they are.

MOBILISE for WAR WORK!

Still ▶ smouldering hours after the last bomber had gone home. This is the Royal Insurance Company building in the city centre

4 The Blitz

AIR Ministry Intelligence had learned form their earlier errors. When Coventry was bombed a few weeks before, they had been caught unawares and had been unable to offer little warning to the Midlands city to take cover. The price was enormous with hundreds perishing in the wrecked city.

December 12, 1940, was different, though the outcome was sadly little different. By late afternoon the men and women on constant wartime watch in the intelligence HQ had detected the tell tale signs of another German raid. Radio beams were being laid across northern England in readiness to guide the Luftwaffe bombers to their target.

This time, the intelligence teams got to work rapidly, calculating the likely target of the next raid as depicted by the invisible beams. As the weak winter sun slipped behind the Pennines, the

The building was just a blazing pile...

suspected target was finally identified. The beams pointed the way to Sheffield, the steel production heart of Britain's war effort. There was still no guarantee that this meant the bombers would strike...nor was it any indication of the severity of the raid which was about to be unleashed on Sheffield.

Past experiences had shown that the Germans were capable of nuisance raids, their planes buzzing over the city to little effect.

While those in the know held

◄ *Sparks fly as another historic city centre building is devoured in flames. Many fires were started by the thousands of incendiaries dropped as a prelude to the delivery of the high explosive bombs*

their breath and hoped that the radio beams pinpointing Sheffield were not the early signs of a major raid (the yellow alert came at 6.15, followed by purple at 6.45), the people of the city went about their lives as normally as the war allowed. Shops had closed for a half day, it being Thursday, and it was time to relax.

◄ *Walsh's store goes up in flames. A stricken tram begins to catch fire. And, to the left, another tram disintegrates at the very moment this picture was taken. The heart of Sheffield became one terrifying inferno*

Steelworkers looked forward to the 7pm end of their 12 hour shifts. And, as evening wore on, the men and women of Sheffield began to make their way back into the city centre to fill the cinemas, theatres and pubs. It was going to take more than a war to daunt that northern spirit.

As a result, when the red alert was given and the sirens began their by now familiar warning at 7pm, the city prepared to get on with its life as best it could. Shortly after the first enemy plane was heard overhead. It was a Heinkel of Kampfgruppe 100, which was acting as pathfinder for an armada of aircraft already making their way north across England. The Blitz which had already brought death and destruction to cities as far apart as London and Liverpool, Manchester and Portsmouth, was about to become an unforgetable part of Sheffield's history.

The Heinkel released a stream of parachute flares. They hung in the cloudless sky, adding to the natural light from a bomber's moon already illuminating the city below. With the help of the flares, the Heinkel continued its work of pinpointing targets for the squadrons following in its wake. It dropped a shower of the incendiary bombs which would later become such a marked feature of the Germans' work that night. They fell to earth, bursting into flames in a crescent over Norton Lees and Gleadless.

Soon the chasing bombers were in the air over the city, the bright white magnesium of the incendiaries below already turning to orange where the fires had taken hold and started fires. The first waves of planes were to continue the rain of incendiaries. They spread a band of fire west of the River Don, the incendiaries quickly igniting the timber of buildings wherever they were left unchecked.

Then it was the turn of the city centre where stores, including the Brightside and Carbrook Co-op, were soon starting to burn. Just 30 minutes after that first pathfinder aircraft had passed over the city the predictions of earlier that afternoon were

shown to be correct. This was no nuisance raid. Already there were a number of big fires blazing in Abbeydale Road, the Woodseats area, Glossop Road, Park Hill, Brincliffe Edge and Moorhead.

But still there was a possibly relaxed attitude among some of those who had visited the city centre that fateful Thursday evening. This may have been because there had been no high explosives...yet!

The cinemas continued to entertain their audiences, the pubs pulled pints and couples at the City Hall and Cutlers' Hall danced as the bands played on. Another half hour was allowed to go by before the ARP teams and police exercised their duty and shut down the entertainments, instructing people to go home or take shelter. As people left the cinemas in an orderly manner, they were greeted by some amazing scenes. They came across the spluttering incendiaries in the streets, appearing for all the world like giant fireworks.

Men began to tackle the bombs, attempting to extinguish them by kicking them or trying to stamp them out. Soon though the sense of the scale of the raid began to grow on everyone, not least for the 400 people who had been enjoying the main feature film at the Central Picture House on the Moor. The building's roof had been hit by an incendiary and soon caught fire. The movie fans were guided outside safely and escorted to shelters.

One of those was Miss M E B Laing, who recalled: "We heard the sirens wail but sat on while bangs came nearer and nearer and then decided it was better to leave. On reaching the outside, we saw the glow of fires."

A commissionaire sent them downstairs to find shelter in a billiard room. They sat on the steps, watching the players, when a bomb crashed into the shelter at the back of the buildings. The cry 'Get down!' was heard and everyone dived under the tables.

◄ You can bet these had sufficient cover. This was the Car and General Insurance offices in Angel Street

◄ The fire services were in the thick of the action all through the raids and after

King ▶ Street was one of the worst affected parts of the city centre, with every building damaged

"I remember I heard a man snoring his head off most of the time," recalled Miss Laing.

She stayed there for a few hours but moved on when the strangely polite request was made: 'Please leave the building, it has caught fire!' She added: "I crawled out and made my way to the doorway just in time to see Atkinson's roof collapse in flames. The building was just a blazing pile. All the time there was the ceaseless drone of planes."

Similarly Campbells Furniture Store with its reputed half a mile of showrooms, became an inferno as it too fell victim to the incendiaries.

Another cluster of incendiaries landed amid the Gas Works in Neepsend and brave men went about tackling the jets of flames already bursting from the gasholders, even as enemy machine gunners aimed at them. The bravery of their exploits is told elsewhere.

It was around this time, an hour into the raid, that the main force of bombers arrived and the real damage, the true carnage, began. Now Sheffield was to feel the crushing effect of high explosives. The city centre felt the brunt of this attack, buildings crashing in rubble to the roadways. Still the raid continued and the bombers spread their target area, sending their deadly loads into the neatly tiered terrace homes on the hillsides around Sheffield: Wybourn, Glossop Road, Meersbrook, Pye Bank, Philadelphia and the Infirmary Road area all counted the cost.

Amid the growing carnage and confusion, the Neepsend Gas Works blew up. All that hard and brave work beating out flames had been to no avail.

One of a string of parachute mines dropped that night landed between the gasholders and exploded with a deafening roar. A mushroom of flame and smoke towered over the area turning night to day.

Despite the early warnings,

which undoubtedly saved many lives as the places of entertainment were cleared before the really destructive phase of the raid took hold, the city centre soon became no place to take refuge. The orders went round that the shelters in cellars and basements of buildings throughout the centre should be evacuated. Remarkably there was no panic, no hysteria. Contemporary accounts tell of men, women and teenagers picking their way home or from shelter to shelter with a deliberate sense of purpose and calmness.

◄ *The people on this picture nonchalantly stroll past bombed out Williams store on The Moor. The way the people of Sheffield got on with their lives in the days after the Blitz was a tribute to their resilience*

◄ *The morning after the Blitz before! This is High Street on the morning of December 13*

A clean ▶
up team
making
their way
along High
Court,
leading to
High Street,
Sheffield

The Moor was turned into a tunnel of flame, buildings burning from one end to the other. From the bottom of the Moor, the destruction overspilled into St Mary's Road and Bramall Lane football ground. Arnold Laver's woodyard also went up in flames. And a mystery was buried nearby. Forty five years later, workmen uncovered a 1,000kg bomb which had failed to detonate. Many bombs which landed that night failed to explode. But their negative contribution to the explosive impact of the raid offered little comfort when all the destruction and mayhem is considered. Hospitals, churches, stores and homes all were torn apart by the bombs and fires continued the destruction, fire crews fighting against all the odds with water supplies drying up and blazes raging all around.

The raid reached its climax for an hour at either side of midnight. By this time great destruction had already been visited upon Sheffield. But it seemed that the enemy was without end. Their planes constantly droned over the city, their bombs tearing the heart out of familiar landmarks, such as the C&A Modes store which suffered several direct hits, bringing the building crashing down on its basement air raid shelter. People rushed out into King Street, some to be hit by falling debris. Similarly the shelter beneath Stephenson's

restaurant in Castle Street suffered a direct hit. Other stores lost that night included TB&W Cockayne, John Walsh Ltd, Crossley's, John Atkinson, and Roberts Brothers.

One of the most chilling episodes was acted out in Westbrook Bank, Sharrow where rescuers were desperately trying to free a soldier trapped in the cellar of a house which had suffered a direct hit, debris pinning him down by the legs. A team of rescuers had just managed to tunnel down to the stricken soldier when another bomb landed on exactly the same spot. A Civil Denfence team took until daybreak to reach the casualties. Five of the original rescue squad were dead, two others were seriously injured and an ambulance

driver had been blown to pieces. The leader of the first aid team was found crushed, lying on top of a civilian helper who was brought out alive.

The Mappin Art Gallery and City Museum were damaged when a bomb exploded in Mushroom Lane. Windows were blown out and the glass in exhibit cases broken. Luckily many of the more valuable items had been removed for safe keeping. In Campo Lane, the Church Army hostel was hit, killing a number of residents, but nearly 100 people sheltering in the basement managed to survive. They were dug out by rescuers who included the driver of the Church Army mobile canteen. He had just returned to base when the bomb landed, wrecking the vehicle.

This ▶
panoramic
shot through
the rooftops
towards Angel
Street in the
city centre
gives an
idea of the
scale of the
devastation.
The gutted
white
building is
Burtons
store. In the
centre is a
tram - one of
the few to
escape destruction in the
bombings

Just before midnight the biggest single tragedy occurred when the Marples Hotel in High Street. The basement of the substantial, seven storey building had been considered one of the safest places in Sheffied. But a direct hit brought the masonry and timbers crashing down and started a fire which burned for hours. An untold number of people lost their lives. Identification of victims was impossible but it is known that 64 bodies were recovered and fragments of six or seven others discovered. However, rescue teams, who were not able to get to work until 10am the following day, did bring some people out alive. They had taken refuge in the hotel's bottle store and, despite a lack of oxygen, managed to hold on until help arrived. The Germans had intended to hit the industrial districts of the city but, partly thanks to the blanket of fog and smog lying to the east of the city centre, there was little damage. However, George Senior and son, at the bottom of Commercial Street, was rocked by an explosion and its tall brick chimney came down after swaying for a few seconds.

◀ Somebody's home. Westbourne Road had its share of destruction

◀ The clean up gets underway. Here the first swings of a pick axe dig into the rubble outside the Empire building, at the corner of Charles Street and Union Street

35

A few hours earlier, people had been enjoying a drink and a sing song in the Devonshire Arms on the Moor. After the bombs, it was little more than a pile of rubble and a few flame charred murals on the neighbouring building

Relief from the bombs came in the early hours as the raid began to slacken off. More people began to emerge from the shelters and make their way home through the rubble and chaos. Few would have bothered to check the time, but if they had looked at their watches, they would have seen a lone German bomber circling overhead at 4am. For no strategic reason, it moved over Nether Edge and dropped its bombs on a predominantly residential area.

This was the last act of violence from the Germans on the first night of the Blitz (the raiders were to return three nights later). The All Clear was sounded 17 minutes later. But it was given mostly by police and wardens shouting or blowing whistles. Most of the city's sirens had been lost in the raid.

A few hours later the sun rose over a frosted city. The destruction challenges belief today. Every building in Angel Street and King Street which had not been destroyed was on fire. Fargate had escaped the loss of any buildings but blast damage had taken its toll. The Moor was a sea of flames, Campbells Furniture Store was still on fire.

In Church Street, the Royal Insurance Building was a pile of rubble and shops at the bottom of Snig Hill were wrecked, along with the Blue Boar Hotel. Elsewhere two of the city's most ancient hotels and inns had been wrecked. The King's Head Hotel had weathered all kinds of storms since the 1570s but it disappeared that night. So did the Angel Hotel, which had hosted Sheffield's celebratory dinner following Wellington's victory at Waterloo. Other pubs to disappear that night were the Westminster Hotel, the Shades Vaults, the Mecca Hotel, the Bodega, the Three Horse Shoes, the Devonshire Arms and the Royal Oak.

The city's tram system had ground to a halt, many of the double decker vehicles having been burned out in the raid.

There were 154 schools in Sheffield at the start of the war. By the end of the December 12 raid, 98 were damaged and eight destroyed, including the Maud Maxfield School for the Deaf. Many of the city's hospitals had been hit, the worst being Nether Edge Hospital where six people lost their lives and the Jessop Hospital for Women. Part of it had to be abandoned, so severe was the damage.

Clear up took a while but was beginning to take shape when this picture was taken of the Campo Lane and Vicar Lane areas. A water tank similar to the one to the right of this picture cushioned a bomb when it landed alongside the City Hall, causing no damage

St Simon's Church, in Eyre Street, Sheffield

◄ Another victim of The Moor bombing. This is Phillips store

PUBLIC NOTICE

SHEFFIELD CORPORATION WATERWORKS

NOTICE

Sheffield water may safely be used without boiling from all taps from which it has been continuously available for 24 hours. In all other cases continue to boil water required for drinking and the preparation of food.

In the event of further attacks from the air: FROM THE MOMENT OF SUCH ATTACK, boil for 15 minutes all water required for drinking and the preparation of food, until otherwise notified.

JOHN K SWALES, M.Inst.C.E.,
General Manager and Engineer.

JOHN RENNIE, M.D., D.P.H.,
Medical Officer of Health.

Waterworks Office,
Town Hall,
Sheffield, 1

▲ A notice warning people to boil water. Basic facilities were disrupted by the bombings

And Bramall Lane, home of Sheffield United, suffered several direct hits. One of them demolished a length of the John Street stand and terracing. Another fell on the football pitch and a third hit the cricket pitch.

Amazingly three of the city's most important buildings were virtually unscathed. The Town Hall, which enjoyed a grandstand view of the bombing of the Moor, suffered only minor blast damage and the City Hall had barely a scratch to show for its experiences.

The Cathedral in Church Street also survived, although other churches around the city suffered severe damage. Among them, St Mark's, built 70 years previously, was torn apart by fire

and the windows were blown out of St Vincent's Roman Catholic church. In Heeley, St Wilfrid's Church and St Andrew's Presbyterian Church were destroyed, along with the Central Synagogue and 61 Methodist churches.

The clearing up got underway almost immediately, with one of the priorities to reinstate water supplies after 300,000 people in and around Sheffield discovered their taps had run dry. But hardly an impression had been made before the raiders were back. The second Blitz night was less severe, but potentially more damaging to the war effort.

On Sunday, December 15, Sheffield had its first daylight alert of the war, possibly caused

by a reconnaissance plane. A few hours later, the alert was for real as the bombers returned in six waves, beginning at 7.10pm and finishing at 10.15pm. And this time they found their target. More than a dozen of the east end's steelworks - and surrounding homes - were damaged, with hits on Hadfield's Ltd, Brown Bayley's Steel Works, English Steel Corporation and Steel, Peech and Tozer Ltd. Luckily the damage was not sufficiently serious to significantly affect production.

Again, the civilian population were not exempt from the bombs.

This post-Blitz view shows High Street looking form Angel Street. Notice that the trams are running again!

Five parachute mines, thousands of incendiaries and around 100 high explosive bombs dropped, hitting homes in Bolsover Road and Barnsley Road, Firth Park as well as Attercliffe and Darnall, Grimesthopre, Burngreave and Park.

One of the parachute mines landed in Coleford Road, Darnall, killing eight wardens.

Two more died later and six others were injured, along with two messengers.

One survivor, who had lived in Cottingham Street, recalled that when the sirens sounded, they headed for the coal cellar, joined by neighbours making a dozen in all: "The raid had begun when someone remembered an old gentleman living alone a short

distance away who had previously refused to leave his home and volunteered to go our for him.

"He was persuaded to take shelter with us, and almost at once the bombs began to fall and No 72, Cottingham Street, which he had just left was shattered. There were 13 of us in that cellar. Lucky 13 indeed!"

Homeless people and soldiers gather round a Church Army canteen wagon handing out refreshments in the city centre

◄ *Bomb disposal teams worked tirelessly to defuse the unexploded bombs that fell*

◄ *A treacherous legacy was left once the planes had returned to base as dozens of unexploded bombs were discovered and had to be disarmed. The notice requested the people of Sheffield to help the Sheffield Newspapers' War Fund.*

In fact, bombs are still being uncovered today

Mr Godfrey remembers

" I WAS four-years-old at the time of the Blitz but can still recall a family living just across the road from me, my home at that time being 241 Fulwood Road, Sheffield 10. The lady of the house, having a premonition that something was going to happen, talked her family into taking shelter in a brick-built conservatory at the bottom of her garden. She also talked her neighbours into joining her. No sooner had they settled down than whoosh, there was a noise like a thunder clap. Her house, and adjoining two houses, were blown apart. Within minutes, police, the Home Guard and a few neighbours were scrambling in the still burning rubble searching for survivors. Just then, the lady of the house, with her four or five-year-old daughter, emerged from the conservatory, shaken but intact. Her daughter was crying for her pet kitten, which was later found fit and well, although deaf.

I also recall a near neighbour, a Mr Lake, hopping and stumbling to an outside toilet, cursing the German air force for blitzing Sheffield while he was having an attack of diarrhoea. They could have waited an hour or so, he ranted and raved, with upraised clenched fist pointing to the sky.

This brought his family into fits of laughter, despite the enemy aircraft overhead.

Another neighbour dashed back into her kitchen to see if her pan of stew was OK. She was more concerned about that than the overhead planes. Yet another neighbour was convinced throughout the entire war that an incendiary was stuck in her chimney and never would light a fire in that house, preferring to keep warm with an oil stove or three-bar electric fire.

Mr P T Godfrey
a four year old Blitz survivor

Many ▶ families had their homes and lives shattered but managed to keep going. Here is a scene in Shiregreen

Joe Castle remembers

" AT the time of the two air raids on Sheffield, the Wadsley Church of England school was used as an ARP Centre and manned round the clock. A large brick-walled and concrete-roofed air raid shelter was built immedaitely behind it. I often wondered why it was located there. Behind it were the front gardens of the six Hannah Ranson alms houses. When the sirens sounded, wardens gently but hurriedly ushered the bewildered old ladies into the shelter to join folk from houses near the school who also sought shelter there.

Close by, regulars poured out of the Sportsman pub to join the safety-seekers, transporting quantities of Dutch courage with them!

The atmosphere was convivial and, on hearing the all clear, all dispersed to their respective beds. No damage, locally.

But I ponder what thoughts must have flashed through their minds on entering the shelter each time, knowing that over the wall was the vast graveyard with, more often than not, one or two graves opened and awaiting someone.

Perhaps it would have been better to have put the shelter somewhere else.

Joe Castle
Joe is a well known local historian

" I WAS 14 at the time of the Blitz. I had left school a few months earlier and was working at a printing works. I remember that night so well My friends and I had decided to go to the Star Picture House. On the way, I decided to buy my father a cigar. I don't know why, it was a bit early for Christmas but I went back home and gave it to him. Then, we decided against going to the pictures and bought some fish and chips and just walked round. When the sirens sounded, I wanted to go home but my friend accused me of being scared. Exactly a week before, I was reminded, there was a warning that lasted all night and turned out to be what we used to call a nuisance raid where a German plane buzzed about but never dropped a bomb. For a long time, we walked around, listening to the bangs of planes and our ack-ack guns. We were just going down Harrow Street, a small lane between Ecclesall Road and Napier Street, when all of a sudden the sky became red and a horrible swishing noise came towards us. There was a factory nearby and I remem-

ber putting my hands over my head and saying, 'mother, mother.' We ran into this factory. A man at the door took us to an underground room full of night shift workers. They were so good to us, giving us drinks and some blankets to keep warm. We stayed there all night. We found out the swishing noise was incendiary

There were bricks everywhere and I had to step over hosepipes from the fire engines. It was like another world.

bombs falling on the factory roof (the men on fire watch duty put them out). When the all clear finally sounded we wanted to go home but first we were made to wait about an hour.

When I stepped out of the factory I got such a shock. There were bricks everywhere on the ground and I had to step over hosepipes from the fire engines. It was like another world. I finally reached Milton

Street, which wasn't as bad. I lived in a small street off Milton Street, Evans Street. I reached it but dare not look round the corner, I was so afraid our house would be gone. Everywhere were sandbags for putting out incendiaries. I finally looked round the corner and saw our house was still standing and just sat down on the sandbag crying.

After a while, my elder sister came running down the street: "Where have you been? My mum's been going mad with worry." She had heard the Star Picture House was on fire and thought I was in there. She also thought it was an omen because I had taken my dad his Christmas cigar.

The next day we went to see the damage. It was enormous. A land mine had dropped on Fitzwilliam Street and a whole block of houses and shops was flattened. Later that Friday, we were just going to have our tea; mum had opened a tin of paches and cream, we tried to celebrate coming out of it

so well. We were just going to start our tea when there was a loud knock on the door. It was a policeman. He said: "Sorry. You will have to leave your house as soon as possible as there is an unexploded bomb in Viner's shelters." It appears a factory worker was collecting his wages and looked out of a window and saw the crater. My family had heard a dull thud during the raid but never thought anything wrong. So it was back to a factory for shelter! On Sunday, a bomb disposal team came and defused our bomb. They were treated like heroes. We all went to see this bomb, a massive 565lb-er! "

Dorothy Senior
may have had a premonition of the raid

The ▶ ruins had hardly stopped smouldering before the rebuilding began. Workers get to work clearing the debris from the work and, overhead, an engineer reconnects the telephone wires

5 The people at war

◄ Still smiling. This family in Shiregreen, were able to keep up their spirits as they posed for a cameraman from The Star

THERE were countless heroes on the streets of Sheffield on the nights of December 12 and 15 when the German bombers set about reducing the city to rubble. A few stood out for their sheer selfless bravery and earned an array of medals which have yet to be matched in the history of the city. No fewer than six George Medals were handed out to men in the city for their Blitz bravery.

One was awarded to Charles Taylor who risked his life to stop the Neepsend gas works from exploding. He was the 58 year old valveman at the time of the attack and went into action

I went to see if the wardens wanted any help...

when he saw that one of the gasholders had been punctured and a tongue of flame was spurting from its side. He armed himself with a chunk of clay and climbed up to try and stem the flame, which was leaping out to a height taller than himself.

He was forced to return to the ground to get an extinguisher and to try a second time. But this too showed itself to be ineffective against the fierce flame. It took a third effort, armed with more clay to plug the hole, before the fire was finally beaten. He and a small team of workmates then climbed 60 feet to the top of a second gasholder which had also been punctured. While on top of the gasholder, an enemy machine gunner fired at them, puncturing the metal around them.
But the men were so intent on what they were doing that they did not even notice they were in danger!

As the men worked, they were forced to cling to the metal shell to save themselves from slipping to their deaths. Several of the gasholders later blew up, throwing a glowering mushroom cloud over the city.

Mr Taylor, who was deaf for the rest of his life following his ordeal in the mayhem, recalled later: "What I did was part of my job. But I want to pay warm tribute to the bravery of those who helped me. I should have gone off duty at 9.15pm but decided to stay on after my relief arrived. First of all, we put out three incendiary bombs at the rear of an oil tank.

Then we saw an incendiary fall on top of a gasholder. I climbed up and found that the bomb had punctured the sheeting and gas was burning at the hole. I went down for assistance and took two men with me with a quantity of clay to stop up the hole. Climbing the ladder was not easy because I had an eight foot long shovel and had to pull myself up one-handed. I was later told that one of the German planes was machine gunning us while we were on top of the gasholders and I think that must have been so because I found a leakage which was not alight."

Also in receipt of a George Medal for his Blitz night's work was air raid warden Leslie Crofts who climbed into a 30 feet crater in Staniforth Road to burrow with his bare hands through the debris to a bombed out house. He created a tunnel, which constantly threatened to collapse and bury him.

It took him to a cellar and, one by one, he was able to carefully pull three injured people from what could have been their tomb. But that was not enough. When he had satisfied himself that his three survivors were in good hands, he returned to the tunnel and attended to two more injured people.

He said: "When the bombs started dropping, I left my job at the pit (he worked at Nunnery Colliery yard) and went to see if the wardens wanted any help. I found there were things wanted doing so I buckled to, but I did no more than my duty. I only did what any other warden would do."

Police Constable Samuel Radford received the George Medal for his part in saving a total of 15 lives during the Blitz. Described by his Chief Constable as an 'extremely bashful and reticent man', he was involved in one particular rescue, in Fell Street, Attercliffe where a house had been destroyed. Several people managed to crawl out with a little help.

But a youth was trapped and PC Radford struggled for three hours to rescue him, working under the constant threat of falling masonry and becoming partly trapped himself on several occasions.

In fact, at one point a fire started but PC Radford carried on with his rescue while others kept the flames under control.

The Chief Constable, Major F S James said that the medal was awarded because of pressure from the public who had been impressed by PC Radford's bravery.

A ▶ crumpled sofa sits on top of a pile of rubble which used to be a home in Westbourne Road, Sheffield

Another George Cross went to Harold Currie who helped rescue a family trapped in their wrecked home. He said: "Most of the other helpers on the job were hefty fellows. Being small, I was able to crawl through places where they couldn't get." The rescue party heard a boy calling for help and when they investigated found a man lying flat on his back with a piano frame on top of him, his mouth and eyes full of plaster. He was barely able to breath. His wife was trapped under him and beneath her was a little girl. The boy who cried out was further away and had part of a partition across his legs. Mr Currie released them all, fastening a rope around them so they could be pulled to safety.

Acting Sergeant Henry Scott-Williams was stationed in the Sheffield area with the Royal Army Service Corps. Throughout the night of the Blitz and up to 11am next day, he was in charge of a rescue party which, on one occasion, saved 13 people from a bombed house. Throughout their escapade, they were in danger from an unexploded bomb nearby. In fact, it blew up shortly after the last survivor was safe.

Sgt Scott-Williams's colleague Corporal Albert George Wisbey, from Bishops Stortford, also received the George Medal for his work during the Blitz. Several times, he was sent out to lead rescue parties and, despite the difficult jobs facing them, managed to rescue several people.

A third member of the RASC, Acting Sergeant William Lawrence Eldrige, was awarded the British Empire Medal for organising a squad to tackle the incendiaries as soon as they began to fall. Thanks to his quick thinking, said the official report, the area in which he was working was saved from greater destruction.

The BEM also went to railway-man F W Clarke for rescuing a trapped and injured signalman during one of the raids. Two other railmen, goods porter John William Booth and railway policeman George Herbert Thomas won the Stamp Medal for Conspicuous Gallantry in rescuing an injured colleague while under machine gun fire.

*John ▶
Flynn, a
boy scout
leader, was
awarded
the Gilt
Cross for
gallantry.
He wore a
saucepan
as a
makeshift
tin hat
during the
raid*

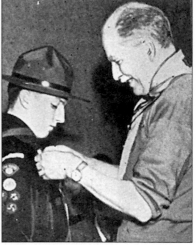

There was an OBE for 18-year-old ARP messenger Dennis Bingham, of Idsworth Road, Firth Park, and a commendation for 16-year-old Eric Allsop, of Manchon Bank Road, Nether Edge. After being blown off his bicycle by a bomb Eric continued delivering messages on foot, treated members of his own family for shock, acted as point man at a blocked road and saved a fire engine from running into debris.

Boy Scout John Flynn, who was also 16 at the time, was awarded the Scouts gilt cross for gallantry.

In a hail of shrapnel, he took charge of a woman who had been rescued from a bombed house and wheeled her on a grocer's barrow to a first aid post. During the raid, he wore a saucepan as a protective helmet.

That was a wise move, as artillery officer John Ernest Radford would have agreed. He was manning an anti aircraft position when he was hit on the head by a fire bomb, which set his clothes on fire. Luckily, he was wearing his steel helmet at the time and was able to carry on firing his gun, destroying at least one bomber which was blown to pieces in mid air. He received the OBE for his gallantry.

They, and others, were rewarded for their bravery. But the Blitz was remarkable also for the manner in which ordinary people dealt with an extraordinary situation. After the attack, one woman wrote to The Star: "I shall never forget the December 15 attack. My family and I were in an Anderson shelter when incendiaries fell, one landing a few feet away. My neighbours' family and mine panicked and ran to a cellar shelter which, however, received a direct hit. When I came to an hour or so afterwards I was buried up to the waist.

My baby lay dead in my arms, my husband lay dead at my back, and my father (who died a few days later) was by my side. No sign of my mother - they got her out on Wednesday.

I was in hospital until Christmas Eve and came out owning nowhere and nothing."

*Houses ▶
in Archibald
Road,
Nether Edge,
after the
bombing
raid.
Thousands
of properties
were
damaged
leaving
their
occupants
homeless for
weeks*

Here are other stories from readers of The Star. They are the memories of ordinary men and women of Sheffield whose recollections of the Blitz remained as clear years after the raids as though it had happened only yesterday:

" WOODHOUSE fire station received the call to send four machines to Sheffield, leaving one to cover Woodhouse.

I was driver and pump operator on the first machine. On reaching the top of Normanton Hill, Jerry saw our headlights and started diving and firing tracer bullets at our machines. We managed to get through to the bottom of Granville Road, where we met an amazing sight. Tramcars and overhead wires were all over the road. We carried on to Fitzalan Square, where the Marples public house had just received a direct hit. We placed three machines on the Moor and one down Porter Street.

On the Moor, tramcars were blazing away, shops were ablaze and an old ex-fireman, a Woodhouse man, Ike Fielding, fetched me down the Moor to one fire. There were wax models of women, with very expensive gowns on, melting away in the window, and old Ike was telling me his wife could not afford a frock. The Blitz started on Thursday night and we were down there until Sunday dinner time when we got the order from HQ that all fires were out and to return to home stations. The best sight I remember was going back up City Road with people lining the pavements and cheering us all the way to Intake.

On arrival at Woodhouse, we went home after four days in hell. We returned to station that night as Darnall goods yard was getting it. Woodhouse machines were out again until Monday morning and the only thanks we got for four days' continuous work was our usual pay packet. If anybody deserved the freedom of Sheffield, it was the lads of Woodhouse Fire Brigade.

Bill Wright,
ex-Brigade "

◀ *Flames leap from the windows of the Redgate store in the city centre. A man to the right faces what was probably the most terrifying journey home of his life*

WE LIVED in the station house at Millhouses. My father was the station master, and on the night of December 12, 1940, things were rather hectic, to say the least! The raid started about 7.15. Amber, purple red came the warnings, and they were here. Mother and I spent much of the time under the large dining table, coming out for a look around when there was a lull in the bombing.

About 12.45, we crept behind the curtains in the bay window, and to our amazement, there, standing by platform three, we saw a train as clearly as in daylight on that brilliant moonlight night, everything covered in white frost.

This was a long-distance train from London to Scotland. It should never have been allowed to leave Chesterfield since the raid had been on so long. Instead it should have been diverted by the 'old road' via Rotherham. Now it could go no further as bombs had fallen near Heeley carriage sidings and the line was blocked. Several local passengers alighted and were soon bustled into a shelter in Abbeydale Road. Bombs were falling and fires going at the old tram terminus. But what to do with the train? It had to be moved, but how?

The only way was back to Chesterfield. Riding on the train were a company of soldiers with their officer, and he took charge of the passengers, instructing them to lie on the floor of the compartment. The train crew were men from Kentish Town sheds, already schooled in the London Blitz and willing for anything. The idea was to draw the train down to the cross-over so that the engine could be detached, but they needed another engine to hold the coaches stationary against the down gradient and vibration from the bombs (this was going on all the time). Fortunately, one engine was in Millhouses shed with a crew willing to come out.

So far, so good. The Kentish Town driver took his engine down under Archer Road bridge so that the raiders might not see the cloud of smoke as he 'fired up' to get enough steam for the pull up to Dronfield.

Then they coupled up and went. My father stood by the phone in his office on the bridge. The signalman, named Sid Roberts (I reckon he was the bravest of the lot, up there in that box, exposed to everything), just waiting, hoping and praying, and then the voice of the signalman in Totley Station box: 'Ghost train just entering the tunnel, they're away, they're safe now'.

Fifty minutes later, a land mine fell in the brickyard, causing severe damage to the station buildings, to our house, and for some distance around.

That train had stood in a direct line where the bomb fell and would have been totally wrecked.

Many that night earned the George Medal but not one of those men ever received a word of thanks or any commendation from headquarters at Derby or Euston. But I, for one, will never forget the night and the ghost train."

Miss J M Barnes

Sid Wetherill remembers

ON the night of the Blitz I was living in Northcote Avenue, Meersbrook, and looking forward to Christmas and leaving school at Easter to start work. My parents had gone to the Heeley Green cinema leaving my sister in charge of us, but we heard the first whistle of a bomb before they had returned home. We had an Anderson shelter at the top of our garden but the raid was so fierce dad thought it too risky going to it. Just after 11pm there was a whistle much louder than any of the others, followed by an explosion and glass breaking. The bomb had dropped in the garden next door, killing two of the occupants in their shelter. It was now very cold with no windows, no back door, and most of the roof tiles gone, so dad decided we all make a dash up to the shelter, after he had rescued three survivors, all severely injured. We were left homeless but eventually

got a rented terrace house in Lancing Road. In March 1941, a bomb dropped on Southey Hill. This killed my mother's sister, husband and their three children.

Their only other son was in the Navy, no counselling then, just a few days compassionate leave then back to his ship.

S Wetherill
made homeless

*Sid ▶
Wetherill
with his
twin
brother,
aged 11*

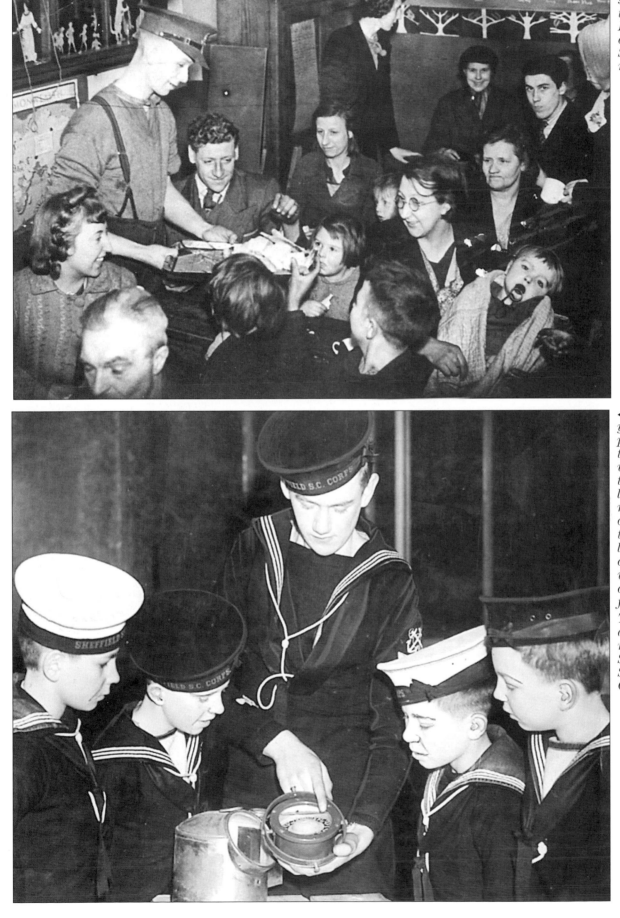

◄ Communal spirit saw them through. Blitz victims at High Storrs School rest centre

◄ Many young people in the forces, with little training, lost family members or lost their own lives. No counselling was available for families.

These lads are members of Sheffield Sea cadet Corps

49

DECEMBER 12, 1940, was my fourth wedding anniversary. What a party Hitler put on for me. Our home was on the second floor of a block of flats built on Crossley's old site on Meadow Street. There was my husband, myself, my daughter - 20 months old - and my mother-in-law. My mother, father and brother lived next door (my brother was on embarkation leave and visiting friends at Beighton).

My mother was crippled with arthritis and could only walk a little, and so was almost flat-bound, and didn't come down the steps to the reinforced shelter underneath the flats, but insisted that we did. My father stayed with her.

So many nights had started with the six o'clock sirens that we all had a little of that 'they'll never find Sheffield because of the hills' complacency, but this night was different. We could sense the urgency and, sure enough, we heard the deep throb of the aircraft which we knew by now were not 'ours' but 'theirs'. The showers of incendiaries came almost at once. We had no time to grab more than our coats. People were shouting, and my husband took my daughter and guided his mother (who was stone deaf and very bewildered) to the shelter. I rounded up my father (watching the planes through his binoculars from the balcony) and made sure they were in their usual 'safe' place in the corner of the room. Father, realising that 'this was it', stayed to shield my mother…and save her life.

About eight o'clock, a bomb hit some houses near the other entrance to the shelter, killing all but one lady. Then, the cry went up for volunteers to help get some people out of a shelter down the road. My husband and some of the men went and brought them to our shelter.

All the time, the building was shaken by other bombs or blasts nearby. Ours came about one hour later. It went right throughout the flats, slanting down to a pub adjoining.

As far as I know, no lives were lost. My husband dashed up the stairs and found my mother and dad still in the corner of what was left of the room.

Dad had a slight head injury and my mother was unhurt. How they escaped falling right down the large hole in the centre of the room I'll never know. All that remained was the passage to the door and the concrete landings. With dad carefully following, my husband carried my mother to the door and then down the steps to the shelter.

I understand they dynamited the flats down the next day.

Mrs M Black

an anniversary to remember

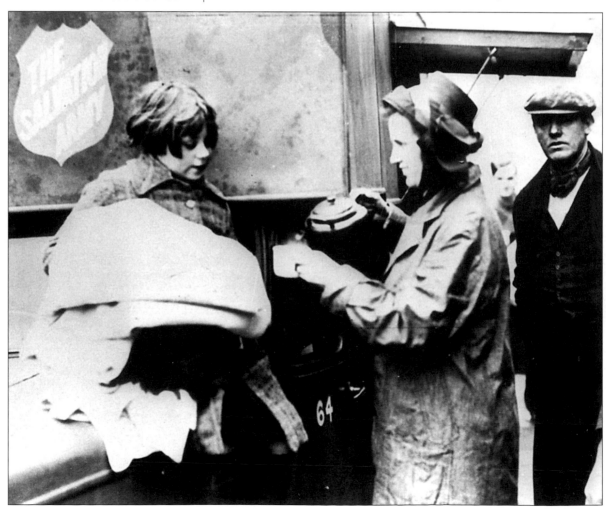

This'll ▶ put roses in your cheeks. A cup of tea from a Salvation Army canteen

◄ *Many people were left with just the clothes they stood up in after the Blitz. Here a reclothing station is set up in High Storrs School, immediately after the raids*

◄ *A great time for kids! Mums put on a brave face to protect their children from the horrors going on around them. But need they have worried? These youngsters at High Storrs rest centre had a grand time*

Doug ▶
Sanderson
in France
in 1945.

▼ Doug
today

Doug Sanderson remembers

FOR several months after the outbreak of war, the bombing and the air raids that everyone had been expecting failed to appear. But the 'phoney war' finally ended when the bombing of many of our major towns started, and the people of Sheffield began to wonder when it would be their turn to endure the horror and dangers of the German planes. Frequent air raid warnings, with their haunting wailing note, followed a little later by the all clear, had lulled the people of Sheffield into a false sense of security, so they went about their every day business. As a youth of 18, expecting to be conscripted into the RAF in weeks, I was in the city on that fateful Thursday, December 12, 1940, the first of two nights when Sheffield bore the might of the Luftwaffe. Studying accountancy at evening classes at Sheffield Technical College, at the corner of Surrey Street and West Street, we students had been informed that should an air raid take place, we had to stay in the building until 9.30pm. Anyone viewing the building today can still see that the ground floor windows are only partly below street level so the classrooms could hardly be said to be ideal air raid shelters. The tranquillity of the clear, cold, moonlit evening, typical of what became known as a 'Bomber's Moon' was shattered early in the evening with warning sirens which ended any thoughts of study. For a few brief minutes after the sirens sounded, a hush descended on the city, broken only by the

distant sounds of the whistles of the air raid wardens as they endeavoured to clear streets and get people into shelters. Then, the faint drone of aircraft began, followed by the distant sound of ack-ack guns as they hopefully filled the air with shrapnel. With all lights extinguished in the classroom, students peered round the edges of the blackout curtains at the night sky that was becoming transformed with a kaleidoscope of searchlights. So far, the evening appeared to be similar to others when bombers passed near to Sheffield heading for Manchester or Liverpool, but the quiet of the night was shattered as nearby ack-ack batteries opened up, followed almost immediately by a tremendous explosion which caused windows to rattle, saved from breaking, no doubt, by the sticky tape crisscrossed on the panes.

This was the first of many bombs which fell during the next two hours or so until, at 9.30pm, the lecturer announced that he was going to try and get home to Wadsley. Seeing no point in staying in a building that was likely to be hit, I asked if I could accompany him, a request readily accepted as I got the impression he didn't relish the journey alone.

While inside the building the noise had seemed loud. It was nothing to the crescendo we experienced on opening the door to make our way towards his car. Every few seconds, a tremendous bang from an exploding bomb threatened to damage our ear drums

and the constant noise from the bursting anti-aircraft shells made a cacophony of sound that brought visions of Dante's Inferno. As if exploding bombs were not enough, damage was being done by the thousands of incendiary bombs which started fires in what seemed like every building, filling the air with dense smoke. Another sound could be heard as if it was raining pebbles. Then I realised it was metal fragments of exploding anti-aircraft shells falling to earth. As my companion edged the car on to the main road, we realised our problems were far from over. We had travelled less than 50 yards in the smoke-filled atmosphere before an air raid warden suddenly appeared in front of the car, waving his arms and shouting that the road ahead was closed and we had to turn back. This caused a problem as we now had to move on to side streets in an effort to make our way in the general direction of Hillsborough and Wadsley. Even when the road appeared to be clear, we had to stop and manoeuvre boulders out of the way to make progress. At last, as we gradually made our way from the city centre, conditions began to ease, with damage seeming to be less severe. My companion, now able to relax a little after what had been a nightmare of a journey, still said very little as I indicated that he should stop at the next junction to let me alight. I think we both knew that luck had been with us that night. Next morning, with transport in a state

of chaos, I was faced with a long walk in order to get to to work at Hadfield's Ltd, Vulcan Road, Tinsley and, being anxious to see just how much damage had been done, I decided to walk via the city centre. In the cold light of day, I saw how many buildings had suffered, with smouldering ruins on all sides. Buildings that had managed to escape being bombed had still suffered blast damage with shop windows shattered and everything open to the elements. Approaching Snig Hill was a sight that sent the blood racing: bodies lying in the street. A closer look, thankfully, identified them as window dummies blasted into the street!

I made my way towards the carnage in the city centre, where rescue services were still at work on the building that had once been Marple's Hotel was the scene of so many casualties.

Walking towards The Wicker, a short distance from the cinema, I came upon a strange sight that only war-time can bring. A double deck tram, thankfully empty at the time, had been sliced in two by blast, with the top deck lying upside down, whilst the lower deck was undamaged with every window still intact. Much of Sheffield's industry towards the east end was spared the worst of the bombing, as most of the bombs fell around the city centre and on residential areas, causing only minor disruption to the manufacture of the many items of war which were so desperately needed. 99

Doug Sanderson
*witnessed end of
the 'phoney war'*

" HE was one of the countless men and women who, following the Blitz on Sheffield, rendered the distinguished service without which deeds of valour or endurance in the armed forces would have been in vain as the morale of the ordinary people would have cracked.

He was aged about 50 with a wife and four children. He was employed as an overhead-wireman on the trams - these were still outnumbering the buses and were so vital to the city then. All told, miles of wire lay in hopeless tangles on the main blitzed routes, worst of all in the Wicker.

This was at the time when daylight was at its shortest and the blackout was operating at its longest. His home was not too badly wrecked, but most of the roof was off and the windows were shattered. His family were accommodated in the basement of what was to be St Leonard's Church, Norwood. This was filled to capacity, with family groups sleeping on the floor and taking their meals on tables set down the centre. Each evening air raid warnings sounded early on, with the all-clear long after midnight.

Toilet facilities were minimal. Like all those with work to go to, he was served with breakfast, and as required, a packed midday meal. The weather was awful for outdoor work, yet each day, without any complaint, he and his associates performed miracles in restoring the tram service.

The electric cableman rendered essential, skilled and arduous service under most difficult circumstances, as did many thousands of others. They would be embarrassed to be paraded for honours, but not once was the service they gave broadcast as a news item. "

Archie Hewitt
praise for an unsung hero

" I WAS told a land mine had landed on an air raid shelter, in a garden at the corner of Heather Road. The family in this shelter were saved, just suffering from shock, but a family in a shelter directly across were wiped out by the blast from the mine. All the homeless were directed to the Firth Park Welfare Centre to be sorted out, and reunited with their families. My father, for instance, had gone to work on a night shift and, as he told us later, had arrived home to find our house demolished. After a few enquiries, he was told a Smith family had been wiped out and was directed to the Welfare Centre. When he saw us he must have imagined we were ghosts, as he broke down in pitiful sobbing which, in turn, started my mother and then us crying. In no time at all, after hearing his story, half the people in the centre were in tears. "

C W Smith
Tears of joy

◀ *Repairs soon got underway. Here two women pass some excavation work in St Mary's Road, which was extensively bombed*

Left hand ▶ down a bit! Sorting salvage the day after the Blitz

The ladies ▶ of the house salvage what was left after the bombers had gone. Their home in Grimesthorpe Road was made uninhabitable but they were able to salvage a few belongings

AIR RAID
DAMAGE

JAYS

Furniture
Replacement
Scheme

IMMEDIATE HELP

3 YEARS to PAY

DELIVERY on FIRST agreed PAYMENT

Still available, splendid assortment of Bedroom suites, Three-piece suites and Dining-room suites. From 10/- MONTHLY

Write or call for particulars

JAYS FURNISHING STORES

48, 249, 250, TOTTENHAM COURT RD., W.1 (OXFORD STREET END)
TELEPHONE: MUSEUM 8255 and 8256.
MANCHESTER, 1 . . . 26-28-30, Oldham Street
BIRMINGHAM, 5 . . . 99-101, Bristol Street
LIVERPOOL . . . . 58-60-62, Church Street
EDINBURGH . . . . . . 39-40-41, Princes Street
LEEDS . . . . 85, New Briggate
GLASGOW, C.2 . . . . 19-25, Sauchiehall Street
170 OTHER BRANCHES

PLACE A (X) AGAINST THOSE REQUIRED

FREE   SUPER CATALOGUE — Post Free

Please ask your representative to call with photographs and patterns.
Please send details of your scheme of IMMEDIATE HELP in cases where goods to be purchased from you are damaged or destroyed by bombs.

NAME _____ D.M. 30.7.40
ADDRESS _____
Post in 1d. stamped, UNsealed envelope.

54

MY sister and I, aged five and three, had the measles at the time and were confined to our home in Carlisle Street.

When the sirens went all the others in the street went into air raid shelters in the works around us.

We stayed at home due to the measles infection, so when the bombs were dropped on the flour mills and our homes, no one knew we were trapped inside.

The firemen rescued us through a window and we could hardly recognise each other because of the soot and the dust.

Because of the disrepair of the house we had eventually to be rehoused to Wadsley Bridge on the Foxhill estate.

This was a heaven to children like us not having seen countryside like it before, due to living in an industrial area.

Jean Shaw, nee Whiffin, Palm Beach, Queensland, Australia.

ON the night of December 12 1940 I was living with my family at 153 Bracken Road, Shiregreen. Father was working nights at Geo. Turton Platts, Wincobank, on munitions work. Although we had a good Anderson Shelter in the garden, my mother chose to stay in the house.

Later on we heard a drone - like engine noise. I do not know the exact time, but a land mine was dropped on Heather Road, three doors away, making a mess of almost all the houses around Heather Green. After a while the ARP Wardens came around and we were moved to the Community Centre in Sicey Avenue, opposite the Paragon picture house, where we stayed until Saturday.

We then went to my grandmother's in Attercliffe Road next to Twelve o' Clock Street. So I was able to witness the Sunday night Blitz from the roof of T W Wards fire watching tower.

George Shaw J.P. Australia

Harold Depledge remembers

I HEARD about Sheffield's Thursday night blitz on the train as I was coming home on the Friday morning for a short leave from Air Crew Wireless Training School in Wiltshire.

I arrived at Victoria station and the first building I saw was the remains of the old B & C Stores. Then, I cut across to the Cutlers' Hall to catch a tram to Walkley - I thought!

An air-raid warden told me I could not cut up by St George's Church and then home because of unexploded bombs, and that I would have to go via Infirmary Road and Upperthorpe - but I was in a hurry then and made my own way. Come Saturday, we went to see if all was well at my fiancee's home, at Grimesthorpe Road, and on the Sunday night I had to catch the midnight train back to London and to camp. How ironic it was that I should find bombing plans of Sheffield at a German airfield, as our R.A.F. mobile signals unit raced through into Germany just before VE Day, trying to prevent demolition of their latest jet fighters. The plans were dated September, 1939, and covered all the main industrial points of the Sheffield region.

Why didn't they hit the targets? My theory is that perhaps Hitler wanted to keep them intact for himself.

Harold F Depledge
found raid plans

NOT STOPPING! War workers have to wait

TO THE HOUSEWIVES OF BRITAIN. In the early mornings and late afternoons your husbands, sons and daughters—WAR WORKERS—most need the buses, trams and trains. If *you* are crowding in, *they* are crowded out. So help them all you can.

PLEASE FINISH TRAVELLING BY 4 O'CLOCK

..and leave the buses, trams & trains free for war workers

◀ *Travel for workers was a priority as more transport vehicles became damaged or unable to travel*

William ▶ Cooper has vivid memories of 15 December

William's ▶ mother, Annie

William's ▶ father, Robert

" ON SUNDAY, December 15, 1940, my late brother and I went to town to survey the damage that had been inflicted by the Thursday night Blitz. As there was no transport we walked there and back. We arrived home in Coleford Road just before 7pm. As our mother, Annie, put our Sunday dinner on the table the sirens sounded.

My father, who was an air raid warden, was working that evening as a plumber's labourer at Kayser Ellison, on Darnall Road. As soon as the alert sounded he came home, donned his ARP overalls, put on his tin hat and reported for duty at the wardens' post in the grounds of St Alban's Church in Coleford Road, Darnall.

Our family, which consisted of mother, father, two sisters and four brothers, practically lived in the shelter, and regularly slept there until my father put his foot down and told my mother that it would be preferable to be killed by a bomb than die of pneumonia or hypothermia! But on that night, after making sure that we were safely in the shelter, my father, Robert Cooper, reported for duty. It was his habit to come back at regular inter-vals to make sure that we were all right. This he did for about an hour, then the bombing got really severe. We could hear what we used to call the 'whistling bombs' screaming down. Every one seemed to be aimed directly at us. The explosions were horrendous and my mother, who was cradling my youngest brother, John, who was just six months

old, expected every second to be our last. Explosion after explosion reverberated all around us and we just crouched and prayed. We did not hear from our father, but expected that he had been called away to other areas to help with the civilian population who had been hurt and needed attention.

At about 10pm the all clear sounded and everyone breathed a sigh of relief. We could not get out of the shelter quick enough, but found that we were trapped by a cave-in at the front of the Anderson shelter, where we had made a wall of sand-bags to protect the front of the shelter from blast. During the raid, blast had blown the bags forward, blocking the door. We all shouted in unison, but to no avail. Expecting our father at any time, we were not unduly worried but, as time went by, he did not arrive. Several hours later, we heard voices, then we heard a shout, "Is anyone here?" We all shouted together and, after a while we were all res-cued.

We lived in a yard where four houses

stood. There was not much left of any of them.

One of our rescuers was our neighbour, a Mr Housley. We had to climb over a parti-tion wall to gain access to Coleford Road. When we got to the road there were troops who had barri-caded off a section of Coleford Road. We were told to make our way to Darnall Public Hall where all the bombed-out people were being helped and fed. My mother asked a police-man for any informa-tion about my father, but he gave a look of resignation and said: "I'm sorry, love, we don't know anything." There was glass everywhere and the roads were frosty. I looked at the sky, there was a full moon, a bomber's moon.

The following day, my aunt Sarah came to give assistance to my mother. Round about dinner-time, on that Monday, a policeman approached my mother and asked her name. "Annie Cooper", she replied.

The look on his face said it all. He informed my mother that Robert Cooper, my father, along with quite a few of his comrades, had been killed during the raid. They found my father's body a week later, still grasping a stirrup pump he was about to use.

Although these events happened 60 years ago, and I was only 10 at the time, I shall never forget that Sunday, December 15, 1940. "

William Cooper
father was ARP hero

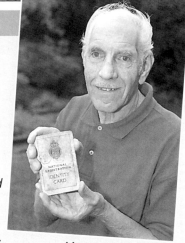

◀ The destruction in the city centre was everywhere. This scene shows a fleet of lorries lining up behind a mobile crane which was digging away the rubble

Les Briddon remembers

" THE Sunday Blitz is the one that stays in my mind most.

When the sirens went up, we went into our air-raid shelter, all but my father. He was on duty as a bus conductor but he later joined us: my sister, Pauline, my brother Arthur, mum and myself.

He had walked up City Road and on entering the shelter said: "May (my mum's name), it's all down. Nothing's standing.

"I think he means business this time and this is no place for us." So we got our blankets and with a family two doors away, set off for a safer place to be out of the Blitz.

We walked down from our home on Gleadless Common to Gleadless church, where we were stopped by a policeman. "And where do you think you are going?"

"To hell, maybe" replied my mum!

What is now the Basegreen Estate used to be farmers' fields and one big field was well-known to us as the Long Field. We climbed over styles, past the old farm and there, right at the top of the field, was a haystack that was to be our

home for the night. We pulled straw down and made our beds but you could hear the shrapnel hitting the ground round about. At times you could even see the Jerry planes and we had a paranomic view of our dear city of Sheffield all aglow. We decided the sight was too frightening so we turned our backs on it.

When the all clear sounded, we made our way home, past the Old Harrow pub and Myrtle Springs.

You had no feeling in your body, only that you were glad to be alive.

Next day I was out looking for shrapnel with my mates and there was plenty. "

Les Briddon

spent night in a haystack

◀ Les Briddon Still has his National Registration Identity Card issued during the second world war

▲ Les as he looked in 1941

A scene ▶ outside the High Storrs Rest Centre

An ad ▼ explaining how to make a bottle to keep drinks warm in the shelter

BEFORE, DURING AND AFTER THE RAID — No. 9

HOT DRINKS IN THE SHELTER

—and the help that is ready if your home is hit

A hot drink is advisable before you go to sleep, particularly for the children. If you have not a thermos flask, you can make a "hay bottle" like the hay box used in cooking, which will keep a drink hot for hours.

HOW TO MAKE A "HAY BOTTLE"

Cut a square of any old woollen material, such as an old blanket, 8 inches longer than the length of the bottle. Line with either thin muslin or cotton material, sewing down the sides and leaving the top and bottom open, to be stuffed later on.

Cut two strips of the same woollen material, 8 inches to 10 inches long and 4 inches to 5 inches wide, rounded at one end. Line in the same way as the main square, for about two-thirds of the length, leaving a flap at the end. These are the side pieces. Mark the main square into three portions. Fold the lower portion over the centre portion making the lower half of a bag as in figure 1.

Sew the two strips to each side of this case, thus filling in the sides of the bag as in figure 2.

Stuff with straw, packed tightly, and sew down the lining.

Make a bag of American cloth similar to the woollen material one, but not lined or stuffed.

Place the bottle in the woollen bag, fold over and tuck in. Roll up and pin over.

Put this in the American cloth bag and roll up again. Tie a strip of material round it.

After the Raid:

IF YOU LOSE YOUR TOOLS OF TRADE

If your income is below a certain amount, you can apply to the Assistance Board for a grant to replace tools essential to your work, lost through air raids.

Help is ready if wanted

Injuries will be treated at First Aid Posts and Hospitals. If your house is damaged, you will get food, shelter, clothes and money if necessary. Try to arrange now with your friends for them to help you and you to help them, but if you can't make such arrangements, you can go to the emergency Rest Centre if your house is bombed. The wardens and police know where it is. *Ask them.*

ISSUED BY THE MINISTRY OF HOME SECURITY

Looking towards Angel Street, from Hartshead. This area suffered immense damage and loss of life

THURSDAY, December 12 1940 was my 20th birthday. My father died while I was young and my mother had to bring up me, my two sisters and a younger brother. When I left school I worked in a few cutlery firms but at 18 I heard that Firth Vickers were opening a foundry on Carlisle Street to make parts for Bristol Hercules aircraft engines. I applied for a job there and was accepted. When the war started we were put on 12 hour shifts, seven days a week, so my mother had no money worries, not that you could buy much thanks to rationing. On the day of the air raid sirens began wailing just as we were clocking out at seven o'clock. I used to walk with one of the lads to Staniforth Road. As we walked the searchlights began to sweep the sky and anti aircraft guns began to fire. My friend said "It looks as if it is our night Harold, do you want to shelter in our house?"

"No," I said, "I'd better get home or my mother will be worrying about me." We said our good-nights and went our different ways. As it turned out I had made the right choice. The blast from a nearby bomb blew down their house and it was two days before they were dug out. Luckily no one was killed.

I continued walking up Woodburn Road and Manor Lane and from there I could see a red glow as the first fire took hold. The Manor Lane gun site was putting up a fierce barrage. We lived on Southend Road and only a field separated us from that gun site so our house trembled with every round fired. My family was still in the house so I told them to run one at a time down the garden and into our Anderson shelter as shrapnel fell down. So we all sat in the shelter listening to

He was a very brave man. Unfortunately he was killed in the Sunday night Blitz

the screech of falling bombs, the bark of ack ack and the occasional rattle of machine guns as the German gunners tried to shoot down a barrage balloon. Our local air raid warden went round the shelters with a glass and a bottle of water asking if anyone needed a drink. He was a very brave man and unfortunately was killed in the Sunday night blitz. When the sirens blew the all clear, we all came out of our shelters to find a world that was white with a hard frost and a big round full moon that looked like an orange as it reflected a city on fire. To say we were so close to a gun site which you could suspect to be a main target, there was not a lot of damage, just a few broken windows or slates off. There was

no gas, so my mother collected some broken wood, got a fire going and soon was giving out some lovely cups of tea. At 6.30am I started to walk down to work and found plenty of destruction. Huge bomb craters on Woodburn Road and Carlisle Street, tram cars cut into two, buildings on fire and no water to deal with them, ARP men and soldiers digging for survivors in shattered houses. On arrival at the factory I was told to go home and report back in two days time as there was no electric power and also a bomb had landed nearby and not exploded. I thought I would go to see how my pal's parents were. He had been called up when the war started and was now in the army, on a searchlight site in London. His parents lived in Broadfield Road. Some houses had been flattened and there was no sign of life except a policeman standing there. He said they had all been evacuated and are in the baths. "And it is because of a delayed action bomb in that house," he said, pointing to my pal's house. I found my pal's father, the women were out looking for food. They came back after a while and said they could not find anything as most shops were reduced to rubble. My pal's father said "In our house we have some tins of Spam that we were saving for Christmas". He asked

me to go with him and off we went. When we approached the house the policeman warned us that we could go no further. We explained that we were looking for food so he said to us: "In five minutes I am going down there for a smoke. If I don't see anyone go in that house then I am in the clear."

The policeman later went for his smoke and we went in the house. I was told to wait in the cellar while he went for a pillowcase to put the tins in. I lit a candle and went into the cellar and there was this bomb. My pal's father saw me looking apprehensively at it and said: "Don't worry, Harold, if it ain't got your name on it it ain't gonna hurt you." He had been in the trenches in the 1914-18 war. "My name isn't on this side," I said, "but I can't see the other side." We took the tins, some mixed fruit and a few blankets back to the baths, and others, seeing them, began going to their houses for food and blankets. By now it was beginning to go dark so I set off for home. Some places had got electric supply so we were able to listen to the wireless. I finally got to bed and as some other town was receiving the Blitz treatment we were able to get a good night's sleep. My final thought was, will I live to reach my 21st birthday?

Harold Doughty
looked for his name on UXB

Christmas ▶
after the Blitz
and a sprig
of mistletoe
means dad
gets to kiss
his favourite
girl. This was
taken at High
Storrs rest
centre

WHEN the sirens sounded in the early evening of Sunday, December 15, only three days after the great Blitz, we dropped everything, left the piano open with its Carols For All and hurried into the rein-forced cellar, to be joined by the neighbours to await the next onslaught. In the short interval before the ominous drone of the German bombers was heard, some-one observed that there were 13 of us - too late for the superstitious to do anything about it, as almost at once came the whistle and crunch of bombs - some distance away, I thought.

We were blissfully unaware that a parachute mine was drifting silently towards us, and our conversation was broken off in mid-sentence by a fantastic explosion, bringing the house down on top of us. For a time, it was difficult to breathe through the almost solid dust, but there was no panic and after a while we were able to look around by the light of a small torch to see that the cellar roof still held, though the girders were bent and twisted. All escape routes were blocked solid. There was nothing to do but wait for the all-clear and hope to be rescued, but during the next six hours, I began to wonder if the air supply would last out. Any attempt to move anything brought the risk of the roof caving in, so all we could do was to take turns to call for help through the coal chute area. At long last our muffled cries were heard by surprised rescue men, who slowly dug a narrow space through to us. We were pulled through one by one to step out into the cold night air about 2am amidst a scene of desolation which was once Cottingham Street.

We were homeless, without possessions but very thankful to be alive.

Edward Lomas
bomb brought house down

THE firm at which I worked was in the east end, and after a 12-hour shift on days, I cycled home. My friend and I had intended to go to town that night, but when he called at our house in Chelmsford Street, some instinct told me to stay by the fireside. Soon the sirens sounded, then the bombing started. The next door house was hit and our fire was blown out.

My father was trapped in the chair and the roof was blown off. If the Germans had arrived any later, I would most likely have died in my bed, as a beam fell straight across it. The thing that annoyed me most was that, after being constipated for years, that bomb cured me.... but blew the toilets down!

Gerald Mills
cured by the air raid

◀ *Blitz or no Blitz, there was nothing going to stop the survivors of the bombings from making Christmas special for their children. Here presents are handed out around a Christmas tree in a rest centre... and a young boy receives a model aeroplane*

Gently ▶ does it. One of the survivors is lifted carefully by eight rescuers who worked without rest to release people trapped in the Marples Hotel. The building, thought to be one of the safest places to shelter during a raid, suffered the biggest loss of life when it was bombed on the night of December 12

6 Death in The Pub

◄ *A comforting word for one of the lucky ones. A makeshift stretcher is provided for a man pulled from the Marples Hotel*

THE Marples Hotel was a popular place. Standing in the heart of Sheffield, on the corner of Fitzalan Square and High Street, it would fill every night. Sheffield people and those who had travelled to the city would mix in its bars sharing stories and reminiscences. On December 12, they were to share much more when the hotel became a tomb claiming the largest single loss of life in the entire raid.

But until that final, fateful moment at 11.44pm when a

His wife was a barmaid in the Marples

high explosive bomb scored a direct hit on the building, everyone believed themselves to be safe and secure.

After all, the Marples Hotel was a stout and sturdy building. Occupying seven stories and boasting a network of cellars if

the worst came to the worst, it seemed to throw a protective arm around everyone who stepped through the door. In fact, the manager had been heard to reassure customers, pointing to the ceilings piled one atop the next: "No bomb could get through that lot!" And so it was business as usual for the Marples Hotel when the sirens went on what was to go down in history as the night of the Sheffield Blitz.

As the raid grew in intensity and buildings round about were blown to smithereens or gutted by incendiaries, spirits remained high in the Marples.

Customers were heard singing cheerful choruses, the staff joining in, and the comradeship grew. Several soldiers on leave were among the customers. They came into their own at around 10.50pm when the C&A Mode store opposite suffered a direct hit. Flying glass sprayed many customers, inflicting serious cuts. They went down to the cellars to have their wounds bandaged by the soldiers, who used their stock of field dressings. That incident probably added to the sense of security. If the Marples Hotel was still standing after a building a few yards away suffered a direct hit, then surely it was charmed, the right place to be while the bombs were falling and mayhem ruling the streets of Sheffield.

Harold Orton, of High Green, was making his way home through the raid with some workmates. Among them was Albert Shooter. His wife was a barmaid at the Marples. Albert faced a dilemma. Should he go into the hotel and ask his wife to leave straight away or head home himself to look after their young children?
He looked up at the towering building and decided that his wife would be safer where she was, and turned for home.

Harold recalled that midway along their journey, Albert turned to look at the growing destruction over the city centre and thought aloud that he regretted not collecting his wife. He would never see her again.

She was among the scores who died. Another barmaid to lose her life in the Marples disaster was Edith Wilson, of Bastock Road. It was her wedding anniversary. Her steelworker husband Thomas had planned to join his wife at the hotel for a celebration. His wife set off for work, despite the interruption to public transport from the outset of the raid.
Thomas stayed behind for a while with a relative and her young son who had lived through the London Blitz and were visiting Sheffield for a few days. The growing intensity of the raid put an end to Thomas's hopes of joining his wife for that anniversary celebration. His prayers that his wife would survive the night were not answered.

More fortunate was Sarah Baldock and her husband, from Jordanthorpe. And they can thank a Laurel and Hardy film for saving their lives. She wrote to The Star some years later: "My husband and I always went

on Thursday afternoons to the Regent Cinema. After we came out, we always went to the Marples Hotel. But the Thursday of the Blitz, the picture at the Regent was a Laurel and Hardy film, and for once I did not fancy the picture. So we gave our weekly outing a miss. I am sure it was fate that we did not go that day to the Marples. Our family and friends hugged and kissed us when we came out of the shelter, relieved to see we were alive. I would not be here today had we decided to see that film."

Certainly she would probably have shared the fate of many customers if she had been there at 11.44pm.

At that moment, Corporation Inspector William Reading, who had been trying to move the trapped trams from the city centre, was in the transport offices in Fitzalan Square. He heard a tremendous explosion outside. The Marples Hotel had suffered a direct hit.

Its seven floors of guests' bedrooms, concert rooms, bars and lounges collapsed into a thousand tons of rubble.
The adjacent building, a seed and nursery business and shop run by Fisher, Son and Sibray, was also flattened.

Searching ▶ through the debris of the Marples Hotel

◀ *A cup of tea and a biscuit for rescuers called in to dig through the wreckage of the Marples Hotel. Handing out the refreshments are members of the Salvation Army*

Mr Reading said: "When I rushed outside I saw that the Marples had been hit, the building had collapsed and where it had stood was a heap of rubble about 15 feet high." The destruction was complete. The chances of survival almost nil.

Yet some did manage to live through that horror. Rescue workers began to claw away at the debris at around 10am the following morning but it was several hours before they began to reach the survivors. These were men who had somehow lived through the most terrible experience of their lives. They told vivid stories of how they spent the night trapped in the cellars, hardly able to breathe for smoke and dust.

These men had dug with their bare hands at the mountain of rubble trapping them, trying to create an air vent. But it was tough work. The air was full of dust and they could hardly breathe. Eventually they dozed, weary from their labours or through loss of blood.

When release finally came, seven men were found alive. Two of them immediately walked from the scene, never to be heard of again. The others were Edward Riley, of Ecclesall Road, Sheffield, Ebenezer Tall, of Shoreditch, William Wallace King, of Bristol, Lionel George Ball, of Bristol, and John Watson Kay, of Stoke on Trent.

Identifying the dead was a less easy task.

To this day, it is not clear how many lost their lives in that explosion. Work recovering the 70 or so bodies, half of them women, continued for weeks. All in all, 64 bodies were recovered and the remains of six or seven others found. Only 14 could be named.

The rest had to be identified through their belongings, such as identity cards, rings, watches, handbags and cigarette lighters.

All that is left of the Marples Hotel, in Fitzalan Square after it received a direct hit. Almost 70 people died. Note C & A Modes store in the background. It is little more than a shell bearing further testament to the ferocity of the raid

▲ *Inside the Marples. This gives you some idea of the enormity of the task facing rescuers*

Mr ▶ Herbert Whiteley today

MY GRANDFATHER, Joe McGarry, normally went to the Marples every Thursday evening. However, that night, he went straight home from work.
Had he not, he would most likely have been buried alive.
My other grandparents, Herbert and Nellie Whiteley, had gone to the Tivoli Picture Palace that evening. When the bombs began to fall, instead of going into the nearest air-raid shelter, which was a cellar in a pub, they decided to try

to get home to Park Hill Lane. As they heard another wave of bombers approaching, they found a bomb crater in Howard Street and jumped in it. They stayed there until the all clear.

My dad, Herbert Whiteley, was a fireman on the trains. He had gone to Liverpool Dock that day to pick up a

petrol train. He was forced to lay under the engine for four nights while the Luftwaffe bombed Liverpool. By the Thursday, all was quiet. It was not until he got over the Pennines from Manchester that he saw why. The sky was blood red and they had to stop the train for four hours until the all clear sounded and they finally were allowed to continue the last 20 miles to Sheffield. His train had just crossed the Wicker railway bridge when a bomb

crashed through it, killing everyone in an air raid shelter beneath. Had it happened a couple of minutes sooner, the Luftwaffe would have found their real target, the East End steelworks, for the thousands of gallons of fuel on dad's train would have acted like a huge torch.

Herbert Whiteley
proud son

Mabel ▶ Broughton pictured aged 12 in 1941

Mabel ▼ today

Mabel Broughton remembers

" WHEN the sirens went we went to our cellar as we had a big Alsatian dog and didn't taking him to the community shelter as we didn't know how he would react to lots of people.
Our house was set on fire by an incendiary bomb and the attic floor fell into the bedroom, the bedroom floor fell into

downstairs blocking the cellar door.
When the all clear sounded, the neighbours knew where we were. The cellar grate, which was in the lane alongside our back-to-back house, was removed. Out came the dog, out came me, followed by mum, but dad being 17 stone, the rescuers had to

dig around the grate to make it wider for him to get out.
Also, if the dog hadn't pinched the steak which was for his tea before he went on nights, making him late by half-an-hour, dad would have been in the Marples in Fitzalan Square, so he had two lucky escapes that night. He always called in

the pub on his way to work for a quick half.

Mrs M Broughton "
aged 11 at the time of the Blitz

Harry Orton remembers

◄ *Harry Orton (right) receives his long service and good conduct medals in 1960*

"WITH the doleful sounds of the air raid warnings (Sheffield had been bombed before so we were well aware of that gutted feeling) whether it be hindsight or common sense our boss decided it was time to down tools and go home to the safety of our civilian shelters, which we had spent much time preparing. There must have been half a dozen of us or more who lived in the Intake/Manor region of Sheffield who had made our way down to Fitzalan Square to catch our appropriate tramcars or buses, only to find all public transport had been stopped and we would have to walk home. In our little group was a man called Albert Shooter, whose wife was working as a bar maid at the Marples Hotel, immediately opposite where we stood. He paused for a while, contemplating whether he should fetch his wife and take her home with him or leave her in the safety of the deep cellars of Marples. Concerned, too, over his two boys at home, he decided the safety of his wife was assured. Best he get home fastest to his sons and console them. As we trudged breathlessly to the top of Granville Road, our natural reaction was to pause awhile and look back towards the city centre, which was, by then, ablaze and still being blasted by bombs. I heard Albert say, 'I wish I had gone and fetched the wife out, now.' Come Friday morning, the misfortunes of war were all too apparent from Albert's point of view. Who could have guessed the horrors that night would bring, for Albert, a catastrophe. If only he had followed his initial instincts.

No use in phoning the boss that Friday morning and telling him we couldn't get in for work, as there was no transport available. He would have soon told us we had a pair of legs to walk on, which we did without the moans of modern day philosophy.

As we walked along Norfolk Street, treading over the debris of the night before, we passed, on our left, a block of shops that had been commandeered to store furniture from previous bombing raids. In one of the wndows, we could see a small flame, possibly an ember from the buildings around. Yes, we could have so easily kicked in the door and doused the flame with our own urine, but to have done so would have been tantamount to looting, so we went on our way to work. By the time we left work that day, those shops had burnt to the ground and with them the furniture stored within (no doubt we did the would-be claimants a favour). Again the misfortunes of war, that the civil services had been so stretched they had not energy, the facilities, or the manpower, to do anything about a lone fire. So, in recalling this, my heart goes out to the civil services of those days who worked until they dropped. In singing the praises of the civil services, one must not forget the Salvation Army. If there was a heap of rubble from which a body may be recovered, dead or alive, you could be sure the Salvation Army was on hand with a word of comfort or a bowl of soup.

On Sunday night, the air raid sirens began again, but we knew what to expect! From the garden path by the side of our house, we were able to look towards Tinsley and see the sky fill with those dreaded flames that preceded the heavy bombing, the thump of which rocked the foundations of our houses. The older and wiser ones who looked on said 'We're alright - they are going for the steel works.' Some among us well remembered when Sheffield was first bombed, in World War One: how the Zeppelin had suddenly appeared in the skies over Sheffield and dropped its bombs in the Wicker area. If only it had been a Zeppelin dropping those same type of bombs, I'm sure we wouldn't have minded. But these they were dropping now were really devastating. Some were land mines, which would destroy a whole area, others were known as 1,000 lb bombs, which could flatten a whole street or 500 lb bombs, which would skittle a row of houses to the ground and, just for good measure, the dreaded fire bomb, which dropped anywhere and set fire to everything. Come Monday morning at work, we listened to tales of anguish and heroism of the people of Tinsley and Neepsend. We also heard the one about the German airman who had parachuted into the midst of the steel works (no doubt thinking his war was now over and he could look forward to the remainder of it in a prisoner of war camp) only to be bundled, parachute and all, into the nearest blast furnace, such had been the anger of furnacemen looking around at their pals, killed before their very eyes. Who could blame men for such anger as this."

Mr Harry Orton
praise for Salvation Army

▲ *Harry Orton today*

Gathered round the fire, servicemen wounded in North Africa enjoy the warmth and comfort of treatment they received

7 Bombing our hospitals

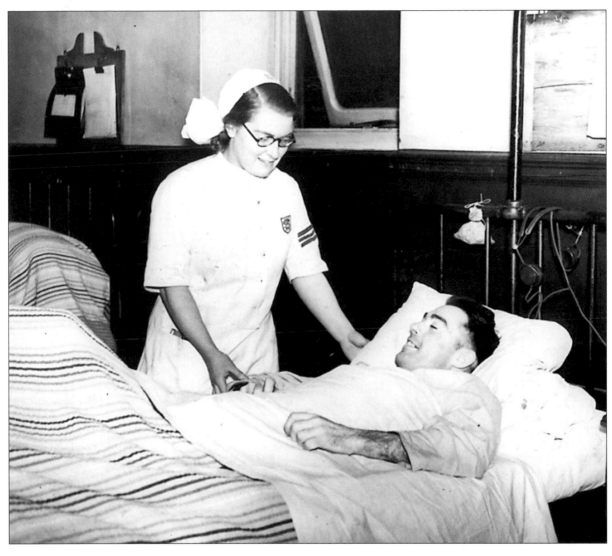

◀ *A Blitz casualty manages to raise a smile as he is treated at the Royal Hospital, Sheffield*

ARLY on in 1940, the Ministry of Health issued advice to Sheffield and South Yorkshire hospitals to move as many patients as possible from the top floors to lower floors. It was sound advice, as staff were to discover on the night of the Blitz. For the horrors of war knew no boundaries when destruction came in the form of carpet bombing attacks from 6,000 feet up. Hospitals around the city took their toll, with the Nether Edge Hospital experiencing the worst casualties when five people lost their lives. They died from inhaling dust after the

The hospital was hit by a shower of incendiaries

hospital was hit by three high explosive bombs and scores of incendiaries. Most patients in the hospital had been evacuated, with maternity cases transferring to the City General Hospital and others to Deanhouse Hospital, Huddersfield.

But there was no place of safety for everyone and there were still many patients housed in the hospital when the raid started.

They included those five fateful patients who had been evacuated form London hospitals. They were in Neal ward, which was damaged along with a dining hall, store rooms and a nurses home.

All the hospital's water, electricity and telephone services were also lost. The old part of the Jessop Hospital, St George's Square, was abandoned early in the raid, badly damaged by two bombs, one in front and the other behind the hospital.

When all the other hospitals were full, eight men who had been buried under debris were treated on mattresses in the Children's outpatient department. Two of them died.

Patients who could be moved from the Royal Infirmary were sent to Wharncliffe Hospital. But, again, there were plenty still in the hospital when it was hit by a shower of incendiary bombs, lighting up the night sky and threatening to start fires that would spread throughout the building. The hospital was saved by a fire party led by assistant hospital superintendent A P Prentice who set off on a hazardous climb to the roof to deal with the emergency. It involved scrambling through the false roof and a dangerous climb up a ladder, battling against thick smoke fumes.

Once on the roof the party set about dealing with bombs, which were still falling nearby. Eventually they were able to deal with the incendiary fires.

They then quickly climbed back down after noticing a string of other fires which were threatening to grow out of control. Among the blazes they had to tackle was a large fire which had started in the hospital laundry. A report later said: "Despite difficulties from darkness, fumes and lack of water, the fires were extinguished and new machinery and electrical installations were saved. The party saved the buildings from destruction. Mr Prentice also supervised the removal of patients from wards to basement accommodation, and then saw to it that arrangements for receiving and treating raid casualties were working smoothly. When the attack ended he carried on with administrative work at the hospital until the afternoon of the next day, staying on duty for 30 hours. It was largely owing to his outstanding bravery and courageous actions that the hospital suffered no serious damage." For his work that night Mr Prentice, of Highcliffe Road, High Storrs, was awarded the MBE. One woman recalled: "At the time, I was a one of two senior night sisters at the Royal Infirmary, looking after 500 beds. I was in charge of the surgical block.

A few patients had been evacuated but we were not really prepared for the onslaught. When the sirens sounded we quickly realised something was very wrong. Anti aircraft guns were firing from Shirecliffe, half a mile away and we remembered that two steelworks were only 200 yards from the Infirmary. We would be a target.

"We were fortunate in having a basement under the whole Infirmary, consisting of corridors, a diet kitchen, the patients' kitchen, three very small linen stores and two sewing rooms. It had been a normal operating day, and patients who had priority were taken on theatre trolleys to the basement. We had very little ventilation. Beds were brought down and crammed side by side and by 11pm all patients were accommodated, apart from two or three who had many surgical contraptions attached and were left on the ground floor corridors. By 8pm we had lost all our gas and water supplies and had to go on to an emergency electric generator.

"But throughout, the patients were wonderful. There was never any panic and we told them we were safe and well protected and the planes and guns were ours. Truthfully, none of us felt we should be alive the next day and that each bomb would be the one to hit us."

The Blitz had one special side effect. It brought on the premature births of many Blitz Babies.

Forty years later, Isabel Blincow, then living at Fulwood, Sheffield, wrote to The Star: "Do you realise how many of us there are who celebrated our 40th birthday this year, on December 13 or 14? My mother, who was expecting me on December 26, stood and watched Sheffield burning on December 13 and, consequently gave birth to me on December 14 in what was to become a very overcrowded Norton Annex.

Blood at the Sheffield Transfusion Centre being converted to plasma prior to dispatch.

I understand that most of the imminently expecting women in Sheffield arrived there about the same time! When I was at school, December 14 was the most common birthdate in the class."

One woman who started to give birth at home was carried one and a half miles through the streets by her father.

He wheeled her to a nursing home on a makeshift stretcher - a door across the top of a wheelbarrow.

Medical personnel showed outstanding courage during the Blitz and were rewarded with a string of gallantry awards. They included Winifred Rose Giddins, of Glen Road, Nether Edge, who carried to hospital a wounded man, whose hands had been blown off. Her ambulance broke down in streets being split apart by bombs. She then summoned another ambulance and carried on with her work until the raid was over.

Marjorie Woods, of Swan Street, Attercliffe, who was just 19 year old at the time, searched a wrecked building, found an injured man and took him to hospital in her ambulance as the raid was in progress. Phyllis W Warner, of Selborne Road, Crosspool, headmistress of All Saints' School, Pitsmoor, was another ambulance driver who carried on her work throughout the raid, then helped at a rest centre.

Other commendations recipients: Percy Heptonstall, first aid service messenger of Neill Road, Hunters Bar, rode his motor-cycle throughout the bombing, delivering messages from his depot to first aid HQ, refusing to rest until the raid was over; Joseph William Simnet, of Musgrave Crescent, Longley, helped to remove debris from a bombed house, even though he was wounded himself; Edith Annie Elliss, of Springvale Road; Kathleen Barber Grayson, of Brook Hall, Totley; Robert John Webster Rodgers, of Aston

Street, and William Townsend of Sutherland Road.

Joan Brenda Sykes, a 19-year-old Sheffield ARP ambulance driver, was based at Pye Bank School ambulance station but went with other drivers to other stations when it was hit by a bomb.

On the way she passed her own house, in Dykes Hall Road, Hillsborough, and saw that it was on fire, but she wasn't able to stop to see what was happening. She carried on working throughout the night's bombing and for the days that followed with only snatches of sleep. Joan was commended for her bravery and she was among those presented to King George VI when he visited Sheffield soon after the Blitz.

Another ambulance driver commended at the same time, Mrs Susan Florence Harris, of Union Road, Nether Edge, was section officer at Greystones depot. She went out as an ambulance attendant, even though she need not have done so, said the official report 'and

set a most encouraging example to the members of her section'. On one journey to the Royal Hospital the windows of her ambulance were blown out. On the return journey a high explosive bomb blew a small fire extinguisher out of her car into the ambulance. It hit Mrs Harris's steel helmet. Despite this she got out of the ambulance to see if the occupants of the car needed help.

Another Sheffield ambulance driver, Frederick Oliver Ravenhill, of Norfolk Road, Park, was commended for his bravery during the Blitz at the same time.

▼*Life among the death of the Blitz. The Star, in January, 1941, reported: "Mrs Evelyn O'Brien, of 5, Norfolk Road, Sheffield, and her baby, Barrie who was born under a bed at the Nether Edge Hospital during a Blitz, while bombs were dropping and the building was on fire. Barrie is Mrs O'Brien's first baby and her husband, who is in the RASC, was able to visit them the following morning. Mrs O'Brien told The Star: 'The nurses were simply wonderful. All the other patients were being moved but the nurses never left me and did everything they possibly could for me. The baby was born in the thick of the raid but I didn't notice the bombs very much.'*

Mary Hudson remembers

Two ▶ photos of Mary in the 1940s

Mary ▼ today

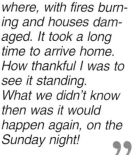

I WILL never forget that Thursday night. I was a patient in the Royal Infirmary after a works accident the previous week, which resulted in an amputated thumb and tip of my little finger on the left hand.

When the warning sounded, all the walking patients were told to take their pillow and go below ground floor to the Sun Ray room for safety.
A hundred of us were crowded into enough space for 40. All through the night, air raid wardens would come to check with nurses that we were

alright. But, it didn't help when they said "All Southey Green's on fire," and your own area had been bombed.

The nightmare ended next morning when we returned to the ward we had left. But we were met by utter chaos. Beds had been put closer together, tables of flowers had been replaced by a single row of beds head to foot the full length of the ward. All around were people sitting at bedsides of patients brought in during the previous night. Dust and grime were everywhere. One of the beds

held a little girl about three-years-old, asking for her mummy; her leg had been amputated. I never did find out what happened to her.

My mother managed to get through all the chaos to take me home, which was a nightmare of a journey. Diversions were every-

where, with fires burning and houses damaged. It took a long time to arrive home. How thankful I was to see it standing. What we didn't know then was it would happen again, on the Sunday night!

Mary Hudson
sheltered in
Sun Ray room

Mrs Lingard remembers

Miss ▶ Lingard in her younger days

and ▼ today

IN DECEMBER 1940, I was at the end of my first year as a probationer nurse at Sheffield Royal Infirmary, but still very junior.

When the raid began, along with many of my fellow trainees, I found myself lying huddled on the floor of our classroom, which was partly underground and reinforced as far as possible. The bombing was horrendous and several major buildings nearby were destroyed, but miraculously, the Royal Infirmary, apart from minor damage, escaped unscathed. Yet I remember being very frightened, too afraid to move, in fact. A few days later, several of the sisters who had been out in the city centre, came

rushing back ... with great difficulty. Many patients had been taken down to the basement, which was extensive.

I remember seeing the early casualties who were covered in debris.

I was very traumatised but had to get on with things. No counselling or post traumatic stress syndrome in those days!

Miss J M Lingard
junior nurse

WOMEN AT WAR

BRITAIN could not have won the war against Germany without the help of the nation's women. They built the bullets and laboured on the land; drove the buses and answered the call for volunteers to defend the towns and cities. Their contribution was enormous. Yet their rewards were scant. Midway through the war, after years of sacrifice and service, women were still taken for granted to a great degree. But a movement was growing which would call for equality and recognition.

At a meeting in Sheffield of the Business and Professional Women's Club, national secretary Mrs Phillis Deakin put the position clearly and forcefully: "Women have been content to be mere slaves for too long. Women must not be content to slip into the back seat they were content to occupy before the war. The war has proved that a woman is as capable and intelligent as any man. It has taken the war to make women realise their responsibilities." It also brought home to men some home truths.

At the outbreak of hostilities, single women aged between 19 and 24 were told that their country needed them! They were given the choice between civil defence work, the armed services or essential civilian jobs. The end of the war found half a million women in the forces. Also their contribution elsewhere was immense. The munitions factories of Britain, many of which were to be found in Sheffield, employed 260,000 women, another 77,000 were working in the engineering and vehicle construction industries.

They also helped to keep the country on the move. Sheffield Transport Committee agreed to employ tram and bus conductresses, and started almost immediately to train 15 of them. Many more were to follow. The male-dominated Sheffield City Council agreed to lift its ban on the employment of married women and the London Midland and Scottish Railway looked to women to fill the jobs of goods porters who had been called into the armed services.

Eventually, as the industry lost 100,000 men to the war, women found themselves training as passenger guards, signalmen, electricians, fitters, boiler cleaners, painters and blacksmiths. Meanwhile, a number of women took on jobs as taxi drivers in Sheffield.

WAAFS ▶
Include
physical
training
as a part
of their
course

But it was in the volunteer and civil defence roles where women made their most impressive mark in Sheffield. The ranks of almost all the teams of defenders included women. The ARP, for instance, had many women in their ranks who showed themselves more than equal to the task on the night of the Blitz. Of three Sheffield ARP ambulance drivers who were commended for bravery for continuing to drive their vehicles while bombs were falling around them, two were women: Mrs Susan

Florence Harris, of Union Road, Nether Edge, and Miss Joan Brenda Sykes, of Dykes Hall Road, Hillsborough. Another 10 commendations went out for bravery during the raids, five of them to women. One of those commended was a raid casualty, a 57 year old woman trapped in rubble in Myrtle Road, Heeley. Rescuers discovered her first and cleared debris from her shoulders, allowing her use of one arm. She immediately told them to stop helping her and search for others trapped below the debris. With the help of her directions, and several hours later, they pulled four survivors and one body from the wreckage. Only then did the woman allow them to free her.

As the war dragged on, it was decided to recruit women into that part of the Auxiliary Air Force responsible for the barrage balloon squadrons. They were drafted in to replace trained airmen who were needed elsewhere. Sheffield's Balloon Centre was to

WOMEN WANTED
to take over the
BALLOON BARRAGE

The nightmare of Nazi airmen is Britain's balloon barrage. That's why it is one of the most important jobs in the country to keep those silver fish flying! And the WAAF have proved they can take over this important front-line job from the RAF!

It's a fine, healthy life for women who are fit and strong and fond of the open air. You must be 5' 1" or over, and aged between 17½ and 43. After a short training course, you will be posted to a balloon site. Sites are usually in or near a town. There you will live and work in a small community of about a dozen or so. When fully trained your minimum pay is 3/- a day *and all found.*

In addition to balloon operation, there are many other interesting trades open now in the WAAF. Every woman not doing vital work is asked to volunteer.

A Serviceman's wife does NOT lose her allowance on joining up, and she IS granted her leave to coincide with her husband's leave, subject only to urgent Service considerations.

Go to a Recruiting Centre* or Employment Exchange for fuller information. If you are in work, they will find out whether you can be spared from it. If you cannot go at once, send in the coupon.

When this girl joined the WAAF six months ago, to become a balloon operator, she was badly under weight. Now she's back to normal. "You can tell them from me, it's a grand life!" she says.

Single girls born between January 1st, 1918, and June 30th, 1922, come under the National Service Act and must go to the Employment Exchange, not a Recruiting Centre.

297 Oxford Street, London, W.1   3010   AR 20

Please send me full information about the trade of Balloon Operator in the WAAF.

Mrs.
Miss

Address

County   Date of birth

WAAF

become the first in the country to be run by an all-woman crew. Within 12 months of the Blitz, all but the most remotely located balloon sites were operated by women.

However, the responsibility and contribution of women was not wholly reflected in their pay packets. While the pay to women rose at a higher rate than it did for men, they still averaged only half the earnings of men in the engineering industries. And it was this inequality which began to gnaw away at some women's sense of justice.

A meeting was staged in 1943 at the Victoria Hall in Sheffield where it was decided to form a Sheffield branch of the Married Women's Association. Speaker was Miss Juanita Frances who said a housewife had the status of a serf: "She is entitled to shelter, food, clothing and nothing else. No man would work for what a housewife receives."

But it was felt the campaign had gone too far when they suggested women should know how much their husbands earned. Sheffield district County Court Judge R C Essenhigh condemned the idea, arguing that women were happy not knowing such details about their husbands. Ninety five per cent of the wives who came before him, he said, did not know what their husbands earned: "The women say their husbands' wages are not their business. So long as they get enough to keep their homes together these wives do not mind where their husbands work or what they earn.

They put up with it and many tell me quite flatly 'it's no business of mine, what business is it of yours?' They do not make these remarks insolently, they are just saying what they think." He went so far as to suggest that anyone saying wives should know what their husbands earn knew very little about working class people.

Undaunted, the women of Sheffield continued to fight for a better deal, fuelled by their growing sense of confidence and accomplishment from the part they were playing in the war. The Sheffield Council of Women decided they should have representatives at all meetings of Sheffield City Council, arguing that they had a right to know what was going on in their city. But the first to report back on a meeting was astonished: "There were rows of bald heads," she said. "I suppose it is partly the fault of younger people for not coming forward."

The first meeting of the Women for Westminster organisation, which aimed to increase the number of women MPs, held its first meeting in Sheffield in September, 1943. It is a battle which continues to this day.

■ Three women who took on jobs as gas lamp attendants in Sheffield, told the Sheffield Lighting Department that they were quitting 'because irresponsible youths had ridiculed them'.

◀ Pay attention at the back. Members of the Women's National Fire Service attend a lecture. The lessons they learned here would soon be put to the test in the bombed out streets of Sheffield

FACTORY WORKERS—
Lend a hand on the land

WOMEN! Farmers can't grow all your vegetables

◀ Early on in the war, it was decided that women would play a vital role. Here WAAFs are learning how to inflate a balloon at the Sheffield repair depot. The city balloon defences were the first in the country to be handed over to women

Mr Peter remembers

William and Christine Peter ▶

William Peter in the uniform of the KOYLI on 17th August 1940 ▼

"WHAT a memorable occasion was our Wedding Day…the Saturday in between the two Sheffield Blitzes.

On Friday, December 13, 1940, public transport being completely disorganised, I walked from Tinsley to Sheffield hoping to collect my wife's wedding ring only to find the jeweller's closed. After many inquiries and having done much walking, I eventually found the owner, but was rewarded with the news that the factory to which the ring had to be sent for alteration had been bombed.

A replacement ring was promised for the Saturday and, having walked to and from Sheffield to collect it, I arrived back in Tinsley about two hours before the ceremony.

My marriage at the church of St John Fisher, Tinsley (which has since closed) was historic in that it was the first catholic marriage there since the Reformation.

The Saturday was reasonable. But on Sunday evening, the Blitz took over again. Early on the Monday morning, because of unexploded bombs etc, we were taking refuge in the church where, some 36 hours earlier, we had been married.

I was due to return to my unit, the Kings' Own Light Infantry, that afternoon. But I managed a 24 hour extension for which I was truly thankful as my invalid parents had both been brought to the church.

We had no honeymoon, no photographs and a very austere reception. But we were happy to have survived that terrible ordeal."

William J Peter
wedded Blitz

Ernest Young remembers

Phylis Bentley who was on a date with Ernest ▶

Ernest Young today ▼

"I HAD permission from her mother to take my girlfriend to the pictures on our first date. We chose to go to the Oxford Picture House at Upperthorpe (now non-existent) to see 'Swannee River'.

We must have arrived around 6.30pm and about 30 minutes later we got the message that an air raid warning had been sounded, but they would continue to show the film. However, probably around 9pm, after some commotion in the balcony (it was rumoured an incendiary had come through the roof) we decided to go home.

On a cold, but brilliant moonlight night, we set off down Portland Street (over which the Kelvin flats were later built) to reach Infirmary Road, where we could see Blanchard's store was well ablaze. We then made our way up Langsett Road, down Wood Street, across Hillfoot Bridge and up Farfield Road where, at the junction with Parkwood Road, we could see a blaze on Neepsend gasholders.

However, we continued over the railway footbridge at Neepsend station and I escorted my girlfriend to her home (at the top of Wallace Road) and I made my way home and spent the rest of the night in our shelter.

Probably we got home during a brief quiet spell, but soon afterwards, all hell broke loose and, what with aircraft noise, bombs falling and ack-ack guns at Shirecliffe (where the college was later built) it was quite a night. One huge explosion destroyed a dozen or so houses at the junction of Wallace/ Pickering and Vale Roads (where the ski slope is now) and not 100 yards from my home.

Surprisingly, as I can recollect, there was only one fatality, but the structual damage was quite bad.

You could say that was quite an eventful first date for us and the start of a beautiful friendship.

However, I wasn't to be her 'Mr Right' but we are still good friends and have indeed spent many a nice holiday with her and her husband in Cornwall, where they now live."

Ernest Young
on a date

Olive Price remembers

OLIVE Price was the first female dispenser to work in the main city centre branch of Boots the Chemist then situated at the bottom of King Street, Haymarket.

" On the Friday morning after the Blitz, not knowing what had happened to our branch, I set out to walk from my home in Darnall, down Staniforth Road and along Attercliffe Road. When I got to T W Wards I saw huge flames shooting into the sky from a punctured gas main and when I reached the Wicker Arches the sight was unbelievable: trams blown apart, half here and half there and the ground littered with debris. There was a gaping hole in the bridge and I could look up at the sky through the mangled railway lines. When I eventually reached our shop - or rather where our shop should have been - there was nothing but broken walls and rubble. All the bottles of medicine and chemicals, the wooden fitments and cabinets had completely disappeared. The only recognisable thing was the shop safe which was perched high up on a wall, blown up there by the blast. Realising I could do nothing there, I decided to continue walking over to Highfields, where my future husband, a policeman at Central Division, lived with his parents.

When I turned the corner of Fitzalan Square I saw that the Marples Hotel had sustained a direct hit and that Walsh's was nothing but an enormous bonfire.

Although it was December, the road was hot to my feet. I walked down the centre of the Moor and remember thinking how curiously precise the bombing had been; there were craters where the shops had been hit, while the road was intact.

I finally reached my fiance's house at 2.30pm to find his parents were very worried.

He should have finished duty at 6am but he had still not returned home. When he did appear much later he apparently looked as if he had been down a coalmine. He had been blown right across the road by the force of an explosion. However I was unable to wait for his return so, after a cup of tea, I set off to walk back home again, wondering if I would arrive before the sirens went again. It was nearly 7pm by the time I reached Darnall so I stopped to buy a quarter-of-humbugs with my last sweet coupons. They were a present for my mother who had been on her own all day.

Sheffield received its second attack three nights later and again I was amazed at the precision of the bombing for it started where it had previously left off, at Norfolk Bridge, this time targeting the industrial east side.

For the rest of the war I was transferred to the Darnall branch, close to my home, but how I walked all that way on that day, I'll never know. "

Olive Price
(nee Middleton)

◄ Olive pictured with her husband, Harry in 1936

▼ Olive Price today

◄ Women workers at English Steel Corporation, Brightside 1942

This is an ▲ extract from Emil Sperle's flight log. It shows the airport they took off from, how long they were in the air and where the bombs were dropped

Flak ▶ explodes around German bombers as they bring their lethal loads

8 Bringing the Blitz

◀ *Heinkel He 111 bombers such as these were involved in the deadly raids on Sheffield. They came over in successive waves, offering no respite for several hours until acres of the city were pulverised into ruins*

And the bombs dropped...

FULL moon and a star-clear night. Only a few clouds in the sky when the squadron, coming from the flight briefing arrives at the aerodrome, where the planes are stationed."

Another extract from another memoir of the Sheffield Blitz. But this one is different. They are the words of a German navigator serving with the eighth Staffel, third Gruppe at Cambrai, in France, who was about to climb aboard his aircraft and set course for Sheffield. These are the fascinating memories of Emil Sperle, one of the men who set off to bomb the heart out of the steel making centre of the British war machine on the night of Thursday, December 12, 1940.

"Charlie, my pilot, climbs into the plane with us and it appears that we are in luck again.

A few turns at the steering, Rudi, our radio operator, tests the transmitter. Chocks away, and through to the runway. The first controller waves his torch - then we are alone. A short light signal and the engines scream. Joltingly, the machine starts rolling, our eyes are directed to the instrument panel, up with the undercarriage and from now on, just straight ahead. Not a word is said. The red lamp flickers, indicating that the undercarriage has withdrawn, we gain speed and height. The first hurdle of the night flight, with the bombs in the bay of the plane, is over.

We turn on course. The landscape below us can be clearly made out. We are heading for the coast. We put on our breathing masks. Dead on the pre-set time, we reach the coast, and our course is now directed towards our final destination.

We switch off all lights, all instrument reading is done by torch. Ahead of us we can make out searchlights. This must be the English coast. In the meantime our machine has reached an altitude where searchlights and flak can hardly reach us.

Occasionally, batteries of searchlights pick out a plane in a weak light. But this does not bother us, as our engines and instruments do not fail us. Suddenly, the radio operator shouts: 'Flak! Behind us at the same height as our plane!' A little gas, and we have escaped. He is quiet again. We at the front have hardly noticed anything. Below us, the ground is foggy, the searchlights penetrate only weakly. Otherwise we can see no lights from the ground at all. One of our men remarks that the blackout is 100 per cent. A few red lights indicate that the night-fighters are about. This accounts for the flak being inactive.

Another hour to our destination. Hardly a word is spoken. All we do is look at our instruments to check everything is all right. The temperature has dropped to 35 degrees and, despite fur boots and heating, we are freezing. My mouth is dry due to the oxygen, my lips almost sticking together.

I indicate to the pilot to lose height to have correct altitude when we reach our destination. The bombsight is heated and adjusted. On the ground in front of us we see flashes at short intervals. Is this flak or are these the fire bombs? I lift the blind at the turret - and there is Sheffield. It is so bright that I can make out the course of the rivers. Snow lies on the mountains to the left. We must steer a little to the right. 'Heinz! Open the bombdoors!'

In front of us must be another machine. Flashes appear in a row. I can already count 12 fires. Misleading flares at the outskirts of the town cannot fool us. I signal to the pilot. And the bombs drop. One of our men lies on his stomach and counts them, to ensure that all are away. We turn left and see the flashes of our own bombs in the moonlight. Charlie asks me for the new course, the man at the back radios to the ground personnel that our mission is completed successfully. With the wind at our back and an empty plane, we fly twice as fast to the coast. However, searchlights are very active again, forcing us to climb higher. The flak's aim is improving. The dark clouds, made by the explosions, are at the same height as us. They are all around us and we feel uncomfortable.

Having taken our bearings, we correct course and drop a little. The variometer turns topsy-turvy and at high speed we fly towards our signals at the coast. One of our searchlights catches us and we give our position and fire ammunition for identification. Rudi, our radio operator, has made contact with ground personnel. They signal that we should fly to a standby station. We change course once more towards the unknown airport.

Trams ▶ *burned ferociously and the heat left pools of molten metal on the streets of the city centre*

After only a few minutes, Rudi reports that he has made contact with the new airport.

We fly partly above the coast, then above the sea. The clouds are very low, but we dare not drop lower because of the steep coastline and the hills behind.

If we stick to our present height, we might get home all right. So it goes on between low clouds and flickering moonlight. Is this land or water below us? Searchlights surround us again, then we see Le Havre below us. Our airport cannot be far now. The time given for us to reach the airport has long passed and we feel something is not quite right. We circle the town a few times and look for a signal.

Suddenly we see a square brightly lit up. To us it looks like a Christmas tree. We fly our 'round of honour', drop our wheels, our searchlights go on, but the wheels do not come out.

We have to make another circle. The motors rev up again, another circle and then we land safely.

The runway is so long we only need half its length. When we report back to the flying personnel we are proud. We too are able to say that we took part and did our best in Project Sheffield.

The good Bordeaux and coffee warm our limp bodies. One crew after another enter the Officers' Mess, beaming. We spend a few more hours talking and drinking until fatigue forces us to break up.

Our group captain shakes hands with us the next day and greets his crews joyfully."

This scene was repeated hundreds of times during the war...on both sides. The air crew were young men, pumped up with excitement and fear and full of joy on a safe return. There was also the feeling of satisfaction at a job well done.

The raid on Sheffield was carried out by a huge flotilla of planes which swept over the city in successive waves, giving the impression below that the attacks may never come to an end.

The raids involved Heinkels, Junkers and Dornier bombers. In the first raid, there were three main groups. Number One flight corps comprised of three waves of 36 Junker 88s and 42 Heinkel 111s. The next group comprised 23 Junker 88s, 74 Heinkel 111s and seven Dornier 17s. The third comprised 63 Junker 88s and 35 Heinkel 111s. In that night, there were 280 bombers in the air.

On December 15, when the Germans returned to attempt to complete their task of destroying the steelworks, one flight corps was involved in six waves, comprising 66 Heinkel 111s and 11 Dornier 17s.

These would have been supplied with maps pieced together thanks to aerial photography carried out over the region by German reconnaissance aircraft flying at high altitude in the last months of peace in 1939.

After the raids another reconnaissance flight would have been made over the city to assess the damage.

◀ In the days after the Blitz, the scale of the reconstruction operation gradually began to unfold. Here is The Moor under a sprinkling of snow

Zielstammkarte (L)

Ort: Sheffield

(Nähere Lage)
N. O.-Stadtteil.

Geogr. Werte:
53° 23' 10" N.
1° 26' 15" W.

Land: Großbritannien (S)
England (Yorkshire)

Ziel-Nr. G. B. 70 18

Kartenbl.-Nr. Engl. 13/1:100 000

E. B. Nr. Engl. 37/1:63 360

fh

1. Bezeichnung des Zieles: Woodhouse Rixon. (Werksgruppe von 3 Edelstahlwerken).

Vgl. mit Ziel-Nr. G. B. 70 17: Atlas Stahlwerke.
G. B. 70 19: Brown Bayley Stahlwerke.

2. Bedeutung: Wichtiger Rüstungsbetrieb.

1. Bezeichnung des Zieles:

a) Verkehrsanschlüsse: Bahn- und Straßenanschluß.

b) Ausdehnung insgesamt:
N. O.—S. W.: etwa 1000 m.
S. O.—N. W.: etwa 450 m.

Bebaute Fläche:
Höhe ü. M.: 45 m.

4. Aktiver und passiver Luftschutz, örtl. Bewachung:

Nächste Flak-Garnisonen:

Rotherham (5 km im N.O.),
Chesterfield (18 km im S.).

Bombensichere Luftschutzräume.

5. Orientierungspunkte zur Zielerkennung:

Eisenbahnbrücke über River Don (S.-Schleife) inmitten Sheffield am Viktoria Bhf.
1,7 km im S. W.
River Don zieht sich in S-Form durch die Werksgruppe, in seiner Mitte ein Stauwehr
(75 m lang) mit Abzweig des Mill Dam Kanals.

A TWO page document was provided to German bomber crews when they set off to blitz Sheffield. It contained chillingly accurate and potentially disastrous details of the heavy industry to be found to the east of the city.

The documents which provided the extracts reproduced here were dated October, 1939 and show that the Luftwaffe had been planning their attacks on Sheffield for more than a year. Details in the documents included information on the workforce (under the heading staff/employees, the crews were given the words 'men, women, public'. War made no distinction between civilians and service personnel or between males and females.) It named steelworks and told the bomb aimers that '0.5km to the North lies the Gun factory, River Don'.

Elsewhere it pinpoints our air defences. The document says that 11km east south east of Sheffield is a military airfield at Todwick.

Under section 4, the crews are told: "Active and passive air raid protection, local observation (watch): nearest anti aircraft garrisons: Rotherham (5km to the NE) Chesterfield (18km in the S) Bomb proof air raid rooms.'

And under section 5, information given is: 'Orientation points for target identification: railway bridge over River Don (south loop) in the middle of Sheffield by Victoria station. 1.7km in the SW River Don snakes itself in S form through the works group (installation) in the middle a dam (75m long) which has an offshoot for the mill dam canal.'

A grim reminder of the Sheffield Blitz fell into the hands of Harold Depledge, of Loxley. He found bombing plans of Sheffield at a German airfield in the last days of the war.

He recalled: "Our RAF mobile signals unit raced through into Germany just before VE Day, trying to prevent demolition of their latest jet fighters.
The plans were dated 1939, and covered all the main industrial points of the Sheffield region. Why didn't they hit the targets?"

One map he retrieved showed nine targets to the east of Sheffield: Smithfield, Nunnery Colliery, Meadowhall Iron Works, River Don Works, Tinsley Station, Darnall Wagon Works, Tinsley Park Collieries, East Hecla Works and Orgreave Coke Ovens.

Today, with sophisticated computer-driven navigation aids, we take it for granted that an aircraft will reach its destination.

But life was not so certain back in the Second World War. Indeed, in March 1939, Field Marshal Albert Kesselring, Chief of Staff

But despite such sophisticated technology, the Germans missed the Sheffield steelworks

of the Luftwaffe admitted that average bomber crews would experience difficulty in hitting a target when flying at night or in poor weather. To come up with a bomber navigational aid became a major priority as Germany prepared for war. The result was the Knickebein blind bombing device, a radio navigation aid which could home crews in on their targets.

The RAF hit back, their technicians fighting science with science. Electronics countermeasures unit, No 80 Wing, had the job of transmitting a false signal on the same frequency as the Knickebein beam, luring the enemy aircraft away from their targets.

The Luftwaffe crews realised that their bombs were being dropped well clear of their intended targets, as they were unable to distinguish between a beam from No 80 Wing and one transmitted by one of their home stations. It was back to the drawing board.

The result was the X-Gerat system. This needed more beams (the Knickebein used two) to guide the planes to their destinations and overcome the problem.

When the planes using X-Gerat were 30 miles out from their target, the crew searched for an intersecting beam which acted as a signal for the pilot to change course and fly directly along the main beam.

Ten miles more and a second intersecting beam would warn navigators to begin the countdown. This was done by depressing a button setting in place a hand on a special clock.

Five miles from target a third intersecting beam would be encountered and another button was pressed, setting a second hand in motion on that deadly clock face.
It ticked towards the first, static hand and, when they touched, gave the automatic signal to release the bombs.

But despite such sophisticated technology the Germans missed the Sheffield steelworks. It is possible they intended the raid to be a terror attack on a predominantly civilian population.

One theory, however, is that fog which had protected the planes on the first part of their journey north, later protected the steelworks, shrouding them in a protective blanket and hiding them from the air.

This picture shows how close the bombs fell to Kelmsley House, the offices of The Star. Despite the threat to life and limb, everyone in the building stayed at their post

The Star

INCORPORATING THE "EVENING TELEGRAPH" AND "SHEFFIELD MAIL"
SHEFFIELD, FRIDAY, DECEMBER 13, 1940   THREE HALFPENCE

No. 16,885

HOMES, CHURCH AND CINEMA HIT IN RAID ON SHEFFIELD

2 NAZI BOMBERS SHOT DOWN
— Ministry communique

SHEFFIELD BORE THE BRUNT OF LAST NIGHT'S AIR ATTACKS ON BRITAIN, AND BOMBS OF THE HEAVIEST CALIBRE WERE DROPPED AND EXTENSIVE FIRES WERE STARTED, CLAIMED OFFICIALS IN BERLIN TO-DAY.

It is claimed that armament works were the chief targets of the Nazi raiders, which, according to Berlin, took off in waves from aerodromes in Belgium.

To-day's Air Ministry communique announced that two German bombers had been brought down during the night.

Describing how the Luftwaffe developed its attack on an industrial region in the North of England, the communique added: "The principal damage was done in one town, where a number of buildings were destroyed and roads damaged or temporarily blocked...

M.P. IS MISSING

U.S. AMBASSADOR RUMOURS
DRAMA OF DUKE OF WINDSOR'S AIR DASH

GREEKS STILL ADVANCE ON THE COAST

LATE NEWS

OFFICIAL INSTRUCTIONS TO SHEFFIELD

THE day after the Blitz of December 12, the people of Sheffield were hungry for news of the raid. The damage could be seen all around them. Most were learning of someone they knew who had lost their life in the raid. But what was the full picture? Were the rumours true as they spread like wildfire through the streets?

Sheffield's journalists and printers had stayed at their desks throughout the raid, only taking to the shelters when the bombs actually rocked their offices inside Kemsley House.
But a pre-arranged contingency measure had to be brought into play to get the paper on the street after gas supplies were interrupted and printing was not possible in Sheffield. The Star and the Sheffield Telegraph and Independent were printed at Withy Grove, Manchester for two days after the raid and copies of the newspapers sent to Sheffield by lorry.

The next morning, the Sheffield Telegraph and Independent could only report, in a modestly headlined two column story, that the Germans claimed to have bombed Sheffield. It went on to describe a little of the damage

that had been done during a raid on a 'Midland town'.

More detail was added when The Star appeared later that day, as it did its best to serve its readers. But news, like food and fuel, was rationed. There was a constant fear that the enemy may learn something to his advantage so every word was carefully scrutinised. However, a newspaper out on the streets on Friday, December 13, told the people: Homes, Church and Cinema hit in Raid on Sheffield. Then, a second headline gave the news everyone really wanted to read: 2 Nazi Bombers Shot Down - Ministry communique.

The full text of the lead story ran: "Sheffield bore the brunt of last night's air attacks on Britain and bombs of the heaviest calibre were dropped and extensive fires were started, claimed officials in Berlin today. It is claimed that armament works were the chief targets of the Nazi raiders, which, according to Berlin, took off in waves from aerodromes in Belgium. Today's Air Ministry communique announced that two German bombers had been brought down during the night." Describing how the Luftwaffe developed its attack on an indus-

trial region in the North of England, the communique added: "The principal damage was done in one town, where a number of buildings were destroyed and roads damaged or temporarily blocked. Large numbers of incendiary bombs were, as usual, employed but the fire situation was soon well in hand. Reports are as yet incomplete but do not suggest unduly heavy casualties, and elsewhere in the region casualties were very few."

▼*Newspaper cartoonists were among a number of job categories taken off the reserved list in 1940 - making them eligible for military service. The Star's Harry Heap reacted to the news - as ever - with a cartoon*

The Ministry was trying to play down the severity of the attack. But the people of Sheffield could see for themselves the extent of the raid. The Star provided more information in a second story on the front page, headlined: Fires Soon Well in Hand, Says Ministry. It read: "Incendiary bombs caused extensive outbreaks of fire during last night's raid on Sheffield and the Sheffield area. A church was burnt out and shops and showrooms were extensively damaged. The church, situated in a residential suburb, was left with only the shell of the building and the spire standing. While a large furniture showroom was burning patrons of a theatre adjoining and in the same block had to leave. An announcement that the theatre would have to be cleared on police instructions was made from the stage. The house was full and as the audience left they were ushered in directions away from the fire to the nearest shelters. Although the furniture premises on a corner position were extensively damaged the efforts of the fire brigade and the AFS to prevent the blaze from spreading to the theatre and other property in the block were successful..." and so on.

Other details included 'a tram-car was hit by an incendiary bomb', 'a high explosive bomb and a number of incendiary bombs fell on a private housing estate on the outskirts of the town', 'a fire bomb penetrated the roof of a public house and landed in the bar, but nobody was hurt and the bomb was speedily extinguished'. It can be seen that every effort was made by the government to give the appearance that Sheffield had handled the attack in a remarkably cool and clear headed way. In fact, the picture which the censors allowed to be printed was a huge understatement, both in terms of damage and the manner in which the people of Sheffield had responded to the emergency.

Strangely, the censors allowed the newspaper to print claims from Berlin. A German News Agency claimed 'that a factory producing special steels in the south western parts of the town was among the targets attacked. It is declared to have been hit by two heavy bombs'.

A fleet of Telegraph and Star delivery vehicles, including horse and traps, motor cycles and a variety of trucks, lines up ready to bring to the people of Sheffield all the news that was allowed to be circulated in those dark days of war

According to this report machine gun fire coming from night fighters was observed.

'The fires at Sheffield were seen gradually to grow into a sea of flames. Many explosions were observed'.

There were no pictures. But plenty had been taken. The censors would not allow them to be published until long after the event.

This must have been a blow to one of The Star's most experienced photographers, Bill Baker. He had been with the company since 1924 and had been on duty on the evening of the Blitz. At the end of his shift, he went to a pub in Norton Lees to enjoy a pint, but as the sound of exploding bombs reached the bar of his local, Bill decided to get back to work.

Years later, he recalled: "I had to walk back to the office and as I walked up The Moor, everything was burning. I was wearing a heavy coat and a cap because it was a cold night, but when I got to the centre of town I had to put my collar up and pull my cap down to protect myself from the heat! It was really hot." Once in the office, in High Street, Bill loaded his camera then, by chance, noticed a cine camera and film.

He had never used one before and wasn't sure how to operate it correctly but he thought it was 'worth a try' and put the film in the camera. It was a historic moment for the film Bill shot with that cine camera offers a chilling souvenir of the Blitz, capturing the full horror of the damage caused by the bombing.

We are indebted to Bill Baker's bravery and professionalism for some of the most remarkable images Sheffield has ever seen.

However, the results were

◄ A knockout idea to raise money for the war effort

mainly to be sent straight to the archive until after the war. They were too hot to handle, the censors decided and clearly breached the rule that photographs of war damage could not be published.

Another Sheffield journalist who was on duty that night, and whose memories have been recorded over the years, was Les Nutbrown, at the time a 16 year old junior reporter. He stepped out of the office for a routine job and found himself in the middle of the biggest story Sheffield has ever known. Les recalled: "As a very junior reporter doing 'calls' on the night of December 12, I was grateful for the strong moon as I walked from Sheffield Royal Hospital down the old St Philip's Road towards the Royal Infirmary casualty department on my nightly check for cases worth paragraphs in the Sheffield Telegraph. The efficient black-out made checking addresses difficult and a good

moon was a big help. But the air raid alarm sounded before I reached the hospital lodge gates and by the time I'd arrived at the ambulance station in Corporation Street on the way back to the office, I was told the purple alert had been received and ordered to return. Seeing the red glow in the sky over Pinstone Street from the gutted Moor shops... Feeling like the Pied Piper as bewildered cats attached themselves to me through Pitsmoor after vainly searching for their homes and owners... And so much more... I suppose the raid and its aftermath gave some of us the dubious advantage of being a little less shocked when confronted by similar wasteful scenes later in the war."

If it was not allowed to publish a full picture of the Blitz, The Star did an important job in keeping the people of Sheffield informed about emergency measures in the wake of the bombing. On that Friday in December, the newspaper reported details of evacuation facilities, an appeal to motorists, and passed on official instructions from the Emergency Committee.

◄ Star photographer Bill Baker, who risked his life to capture the Blitz on film

Here is the text of those articles:

City Evacuation Facilities:
Announcing extensions of evacuation scheme, Sheffield Emergency Committee stated that billeting certificates and travel vouchers will be issued at Central Library to mothers with children of school age, to aged and infirm persons, including blind who live in any part of city who have made or can make private arrangements to be received in reception or neutral area. Similar facilities desired by expectant mothers are available at Maternity and Child Welfare Centre, Orchard Place.

Sheffield Appeal to Motorists:
Sheffield Emergency Committee stated:- No rent and rates are payable by householders in respect of houses rendered uninhabitable until such time as habitability of houses is restored. Owner-drivers of private cars willing to place their services and cars at disposal of local authority for urgent duty are asked to report at once to Education Office, Leopold Street. Free petrol will be supplied while engaged on this work.

Official Instructions to Sheffield:
Sheffield Emergency Committee issued following instructions today. Rationing suspended up to today week, inclusive in Sheffield. The retailers must not refuse rationed goods to unregistered customers. Further statement on replacement of destroyed ration books later. Drink only water and milk that has been boiled. Central Information Bureau has opened at Central Library. It is desired to make an appeal to public to avoid those parts of the city where their presence is likely to hamper various work.

As can be seen, the news may have been rationed. But anyone capable of reading between the lines could see that Sheffield had faced and was dealing with a major catastrophe.

Another way for news to travel in those dark days of the Blitz was by telegram. But the telegram boys earned themselves a reputation for bringing bad news. In fact, the sight of a smartly dressed and stone faced telegram boy on the doorstep of a woman whose husband was away fighting the war was often enough to bring on a faint.

During the Blitz itself, these young lads (they were little more than children aged 14 to 16) showed great bravery and determination to carry their messages about the city.
On the morning after the raid, every single telegram boy reported for duty and, even as the city burned about them, they abandoned their bikes and headed out on foot across the ruins.

The Star GREEN UN

Owing to the Suspension of Sport "The Star Green 'Un" will not be published until further notice

Mr Priestley remembers

“ SUMMER of 1940 found us stationed in quiet Devon after evacuation from Dunkirk. We had moved there ready for the anticipated invasion.

On December 10, I was home on seven days' leave in time for the December 12 air raid. Leaving the Heeley Palace at 10pm, two women rushed from a house in nearby Oak Street, asking me to help

them to a shelter. After a near miss, this was accomplished. The warden told me to stay also, as by then it was obvious it was our turn.

Getting back home, I found the rest of my family in the Anderson Shelter. Our next door neighbour's house had been hit, though they were also in the shelter.

The next day, we were ordered out because of an unexploded bomb. We spent two nights in Anns Road school shelter. I'd booked to see Henry Hall, too, at the Empire. I was happy to return from this to quiet Devon.

◀ Harry Priestley today

Further service in India and Burma for nearly four years followed. I returned in November 1945 but the scars of that Blitz night were still there to be seen! ”

Mr H Priestley
on leave

◀ Harry (right) pictured in France in 1940.

89

One ex-telegram boy, Kenneth Foster campaigned after the war to have the work of the telegram boys acknowledged. He said: "There were about 50 of us and on the morning after the bombing we were the only means of civilian communication. Many of the lads climbed over rubble and braved unexploded bombs to deliver messages from the outside world and to collect messages from survivors to their relatives."

Their task was often unpleasant but the messenger boys, under the leadership of inspectors George Webb, Fred Holland and Jim Taylor, said they were mainly untouched by the bad news they had to deliver. One telegram boy was Albert Bower, who spent the night in a shelter after being caught at night school when the raiders struck. He was more worried, though, about getting to work on time the next morning. He said: "We had to be at work by nine and I wanted to go home first to get a quick wash and brush up. When we got to the top of East Bank Road we looked back to see the city burning. You got the impression that the whole of Sheffield was on fire. It was only when daylight came that we realised the full extent of the damage but we were all at our posts at the usual time, ready to make our deliveries."

Bill Crookes remembers

Bill ▶
Crookes
today

" A BLOCK of tenements in Hanover Street, opposite St Silas's Church, was burning fiercely. On Moore Street, on the opposite side of the street to Olga's grandfather's house a land mine had landed which left a crater 70ft wide and 20ft deep. His house was not touched, the blast apparently had gone straight upwards. All the top left side of Lawson Street, opposite our house and passage, was completely demolished by a direct hit. A family of five was killed. Their dog Bruce was killed, and left on the top of the rubble for days. The bomb also badly damaged No 1, Lawson Street, where my uncle Tom and auntie Nellie Barthorpe lived with Peter and Molly.

That night, at the posh end of town, Greenhill, lived Jean Handley, later to be a friend of ours. She was buried alive, along with her two brothers, mother and father, after their house suffered a direct hit. They were buried for about five hours, unable to move a limb.

Mr Handley shouted for help for hours. There were no sounds from around him, eight-year-old Jean was trapped, with her face bent upwards and a steady trickle of dirt and debris falling into her eyes and mouth, so she wasn't saying much and could not call out. The other three were unconscious or dead. There was only the sound of bombs still falling and noise of debris settling. He did not know if anyone would hear or if there was anyone to hear. Eventually, they were dug out and rescued by a Mr Harry Currie, who was later awarded the George Medal for his bravery. Jean was blinded for about four days, due to debris in her eyes. The local GP took her into his home and tended to her injuries. Her mother was taken to hospital, where she remained unconscious for three days with one of her sons who had a broken hip. Jean's dad had stayed behind seeing to Jean and had missed the ambulance's departure and consequently did not know where they had been taken. He spent the next few days walking round the city in odd shoes that didn't fit, since he had lost everything except what he stood up in, visiting the hospitals asking if anyone knew of their whereabouts. He found them, days later, at the Northern General Hospital. Their other son, nine-years-old, had been found dead when finally pulled out.

On the night of the Sunday Blitz, Harold Wickham was preaching the gospel at Cemetery Road Meeting Hall. As the sirens sounded, the offer was made to everyone either to go home or go down to the lower hall and stay as long as it might take. Most of the congregation stayed on, Harold's sermon came to a length y drawn-out conclusion, still the guns roared and the bombs dropped. Harold recorded later they then continued to sing hymns and choruses until the all clear sounded when everyone made their way home on foot, even though some were by this time a little hoarse and could have given the weaker ones a ride.

The following weeks were chaotic. Soon the Army was brought in to help clear up the streets. Joan, with the help of aunt Nellie and several neighbours, set up a table on the front door step serving tea, supplied by the Army, as our rations would not stretch to this. The 'surplus' tea and sugar came in useful for months! "

Bill Crookes

Reg Munn remembers

" I missed the Blitz! On December13 I was on Ground Defence duty at RAF Wilmslow when I heard that Sheffield had been bombed. The fact that the BBC mentioned the city meant it had been a bad raid. As soon as I came off duty at 4 pm I made for home without asking for leave. Hitch hiking was the common mode of transport for servicemen, so it was a car into Manchester, then the back of a lorry going over Woodhead to Sheffield. Travelling between the Flouch and Stocksbridge a number of Huddersfield based Auxilliary Fire Engines passed making their way home after helping out in Sheffield. I got off in Middlewood and walked home to Longley.

My parents and my two brothers were safe, although shaken. My mother was convinced there was nothing left of Sheffield. That evening was quiet, so having satisfied

myself that all was well at home, the priority was for me to get back for my 24 hour stint on the guns before I was missed. I set off early afternoon to make for Manchester Road for a lift over the Snake. No public

transport so I begged a ride in a car going towards town. It turned out to be quite an obstacle race, having to go through the back streets of Pitsmoor and Burngreave, finally coming to a halt before the Wicker.

On foot through the Wicker, Waingate and High Street I saw all the devastation to the shops and trams. In High Street it was a case of stepping over fire hose after fire hose. On the Manchester Road

at last I was lucky to be picked up by a sports car driver who took me right to our camp gates in Wilmslow.

I of course was safely out of the way when the next raid came on the Sunday. Manchester was bombed shortly after, but instead of seeing some action, fate moved me to another safe haven, at RAF Cranwell. We must never forget that hardworking civilians at home bore so much, while some servicemen like me, at least at that time, were having an easier time. "

Reg Munn
seving with RAF

The city's telephone network was another casualty in the effort to keep the lines of communication open. Engineers turned up in their spare time to man the telephone exchange at the height of the raid and keep the system functioning. One man whose work in this area stood out was Arthur Herbert White, chief inspector in Sheffield Post Office engineering department. After rushing to the telephone exchange to make sure everything was alright, he braved the bombs to make a tour on foot of the department's garages to ensure that all possible steps had been taken to safeguard vehicles. When he heard that one of the

exchanges in the suburbs was in trouble, he and a driver went there in a Post Office van. He had several narrow escapes, including the time when a piece of masonry was blown into the room where he was working and, on two occasions, having splinters and flying masonry hit his van. For his efforts, he was awarded the British Empire Medal. Its notation said: "Although not on duty, Mr White left his home at the beginning of the raid. He visited post office buildings and took measures to ensure the maintenance of services. The courage and zeal displayed by him were of the highest order."

The ▶ Central Picture House, where people stayed on to watch the movie while the bombs dropped and only evacuated when the roof caught fire

9 The shows must go on!

ONE clear message coming down through the years is that, at least up until the Blitz, the people of Sheffield were not going to let the war spoil their fun. On the night of December 12, the city centre cinemas, ball-rooms and theatres were full as they were on most Thursday nights. The entertainment offered much needed relief from the difficult times brought by rationing and shortages as well as the round the clock shifts needed to keep the steelworks operating to satisfy the hunger for armaments.

At first war had put an end to such entertainment as the people of Sheffield were enjoying on the night of the first Blitz. In 1939, a ban was placed on people gathering in large numbers. Immediately the theatres, cinemas and other places of entertainment closed for what some feared would be the duration of the fighting. In Sheffield, this came into effect on September 5 when city magistrates passed the necessary ruling and theatres and cinemas were closed 'until further notice'. After a week of kicking their artistic heels, the ladies and gentlemen of the Sheffield Repertory Company packed their costumes and scripts and moved to the Little Theatre, in Southport. This was considered to be a safe area and not one likely to be targeted by the enemy. Therefore rules and regulations about large numbers of people gathering together were not as tight.

As it happens, the actors need not have worried unduly. The ban lasted less than a fortnight. No bombs had fallen, no Germans had set the Swastika fluttering from the town hall. And common sense prevailed: now more than ever was there a need for some kind of light entertainment for the public.

Cinemas were filling

The Lyceum is believed to have been the first off the mark in bringing entertainment back into the lives of the people of Sheffield. On September 15, the theatre reopened with Harry Hanson's Court Players staging French Without Tears. The Empire opened with a bill including Clapham and Dwyer, Elsie and Doris Waters, Ronald

Frankeau and 'Monsewer' Eddie Gray. Elsewhere the cinemas soon had their projectors working again after an agreement was reached that in the event of an air raid, an announcement would be made from the stage, or flashed on to the cinema screen. This would give members of the audience the option of heading for a shelter or staying in their seats and enjoying the rest of the movie. The threat of being caught inside a dark, soundproof building during an air raid was not enough to keep the people of Sheffield at home and soon the managers of cinemas and theatres were reporting how pleased they were with their audience figures. Even Sheffield Repertory Company returned home on November 20.

But it was a grim time for buskers. A new regulation decreed 'no person shall, within hearing of the general public, sound, or cause, or permit to be sounded, any siren, hooter, whistle, rattle, bell, horn, gong, or other like instrument.' As one policeman remarked: "Nobody shall make any unusual noise out in the open."

For the following 12 months, people vowed: "To hell with Hitler. I'm going to the pictures!" And so on the night of the Blitz, the cinemas were filling in the early evening and the warnings flashed on the screen when the air raid sirens sounded outside. Most continued to watch the movies until it became clear that this was no ordinary raid. This was the Big One! Of course, they already knew that at the Central Cinema where the roof caught fire and 400 people left in an orderly manner making their way to the safety of shelters. That presence of mind, which was repeated in evacuating theatres and cinemas throughout Sheffield, probably saved many lives.

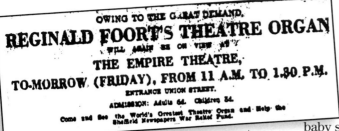
After the raid, it was a different matter. Several cinemas had been damaged. Besides there was more now on people's minds than enjoying themselves. This was now a matter of survival. And it was not just the men and women of Sheffield and South Yorkshire who had been plunged unceremoniously into war. So too had the performers who had been engaged in the region at the time of the Blitz. Many members of the casts for the two pantomimes being performed in the city found they had been bombed out of their lodgings. Yet both companies decided that the shows - Cinderella and Mother Goose - must go on. And go on they did! The company planning to present Cinderella at the Sheffield Empire moved to Manchester and travelled over the Pennines for their performances. Opening night was delayed two days...until Boxing Day. The cast was led by Jack Buchanan, who played his own special part in one Sheffield woman's Blitz night adventure!

Ethel Vick (nee Filere) had taken her baby son to the home of friends in Abbey Lane and had just arrived home in Abbeydale Road, through the 'lovely moonlit night', when the sirens sounded. She recalled: "After a couple of hours my house caught fire, and windows were blown out. I managed to reach the doorway, crawling on my hands and knees with my baby underneath my body. It was some way to an air raid shelter - a nightmare, with planes droning like flies above. I had almost reached the shelter when the blast form a bomb blew me almost into the shelter. Fortunately, I was only shocked and my baby slept through the whole night.

"My home was completely demolished and there I was with no hat or coat and only slippers on, so I hitched a lift with a very kind lorry driver on to the Barnsley-Sheffield road. He took me as far as he could, then I saw a Daimler car approaching whereupon I stood in the middle of the road, holding my baby boy. The chauffeur pulled up and, much to my surprise, out stepped Mr Jack Buchanan, who had been at the Sheffield Empire. He gave me a lift as far as Worsbrough Dale, where I knocked at the door of a house, distressed and cold, not knowing the people inside. I was immediately taken in and given a cold meal, a change of clothing and attention for my baby.

"Needless to say, we stayed about nine months with these lovely people from the mining community, until I was able to find a home again. I shall never forget their kindness."

As Christmas approached a restaurant was set up in the City Hall and, on December 25, a thousand people were treated to a festive meal they thought they would have missed that year. On the menu was soup (costing 1d), stewed steak or roast lamb with peas and potatoes (6d), rice pudding or apples and custard (2d) and tea at three ha'pence a mug.

Seven months after the Blitz, the story of an enduring mystery was published. The 45 year old vaudeville performer Edward Kerford had not been seen since the night of the raid, it was announced in July, 1941. Mr Kerford, a comedy juggler, worked under the name Moir, as part of a double act, Verek and Moir. On the night of the attack, he was appearing at a theatre on a bill topped by Henry Hall and his Band.

The last words heard from him as he left the theatre to head for his lodgings were: "Cheerio, lads. I think I'll get to the digs." After that, no sight nor word had been learned of Edward Kerford. His lodgings in St Mary's Road were reduced to ruins.

After seven months of worry, his wife accepted that her husband was dead. From her home in Manchester she said she could not imagine her husband walking out on her and their two daughters, nor of him quitting the entertainment world.

In the months to follow, the people of Sheffield were treated to plenty of big names to help them regain their confidence in the pleasures of live entertainment, and to draw them back to the theatres and once again declare: "To hell with Hitler!"

Britain's top box office attraction Geroge Formby was in Sheffield in June the year after the Blitz for a matinee at the Regent Cinema, which raised £1,200 for the Lord Mayor's Air Raid Fund. He joked to the audience: "I used to come to Sheffield before the war and earn big money. It was so big, I was paid in five bob pieces!"

Wilfred Pickles was compere for a programme broadcast from the City Memorial Hall for the BBC series We Speak for Ourselves. It featured around 100 Sheffield people. And Vivien Leigh appeared at the Lyceum in The Doctor's Dilemma..

AS with films, plays and shows, so sport also found itself offside during the war. On September 7 professional football was banned in all areas where it was feared the Germans may mount bombing raids. This included football crazy Sheffield. But the city's soccer fans were not to be totally deprived. Barnsley and Chesterfield were said to be in safe, or neutral, zones so matches were allowed at their grounds and on September 12, Sheffield United, which had been promoted from Second Division the previous season, played a friendly against Chesterfield.

Three weeks after the outbreak of the war, the Football Association allowed competitive football to restart, but under different regulations. Out went the old divisions and clubs were to play on a regional basis to minimise travelling. A limit of 8,000 was also placed on attendances. However, when the new-look games were re-started in October, attendances were poor. Just 3,669 people turned up at Hillsborough to see the Owls beat Huddersfield Town in a goal-laden 5-4 match.

Another novel move was to allow players to compete for more than one club. The idea was to allow men to represent clubs closest to their camps in the event of them being called up for service. As a consequence, Aldershot quickly became a team to be reckoned with! Wednesday picked up Walter Boyes, from Everton. He was home for the Christmas period of 1939 and staying in his native Sheffield. The crowd limit was raised in mid-October to 15,000 spectators but attendances were still poor. This was not the case on Christmas Day, 1939, though. On that day, Sheffield Wednesday travelled across the city to Bramall Lane for a derby match against arch-rivals Sheffield United. It was a sell out, with 500 turned away. For the record, the Blades won 2-1. A year later on Christmas Day, the fixture was repeated, this time at Hillsborough. But in the wake of the Blitz, the hunger for football was drawn from the city. Just 6,000 people turned out for a goal-less draw. The game marked 50 years of matches between the two teams and was the 143rd time they had played. But it must be said that both teams were doing their bit for the war, with players in away in the forces. In April, Wednesday was down to a squad of just 12 professionals, all others having been called up. And when United took on Doncaster Rovers in September, both of the Blades' full backs were unavailable. A team trainer Reg Wright and a youngster by the name of Harry Latham were recruited.

J Woodrow remembers

"On the cold, moonlit night of December 12, two strangers and myself took 10 hours to walk from Sheffield centre to Hillsborough in what I could say was like walking through hell itself. Every step could have been our last. We moved through the centre of Sheffield as fast as we could. We saw some terrible sights - like the tram car with the people still sitting in their seats, dead from the bomb blasts; High Street a mass of flames, with the firemen high up on turntable ladders, a fine target for the bombers droning above; the noise of bombers' engines was to be with us for eight hours.

Between midnight and two o'clock, the raid was at its worst, and we were near Neepsend gas tanks which were going up in flames. We did not linger long there. We found a huge crater near Wood Street and went and sat at the bottom of it, feeling safe that two bombs cannot fall in the same place twice. But the cold was too much and we moved on until we came to Hillsborough Corner.

There, we found a mobile Bofors gun crew brewing up some tea. They told us they had run out of shells. Every shop window on the corner had been blown out by a land mine in Hawsley Avenue which, when we saw it afterwards, looked as if a huge hand had flattened all the street. They did not know how many people were trapped or dead. I arrived home as the 'all clear' was going - a red dawn from fires burning in Sheffield.

Some night to remember for a 17 year-old boy who only went out for a quiet night at the cinema, and I never did see the end of the picture as the screen was torn to bits in front of our eyes."

J Woodrow

Sydney Middleton remembers

Sydney Middleton pictured in 1943 soon after being called Up

Sydney Middleton as he is today pictured at home in Sheffield with his old Skill At Arms Record Book from his days in the Services

Sydney and his daughter Ella Heywood who was just six months old during the Sheffield Blitz withy one of Syd's old photographs

"I WAS helping to put on a concert show on behalf of the Home Guard in the Montgomery Hall on the Thursday night. We heard the sirens go about 7 o'clock but it was still decided to start the show. We heard plenty of noise outside and at about 8.30pm the show was stopped and the audience was told that if they wished they could shelter in the basement, as it was safer there than going out into the streets.

Although it was not an official air raid shelter, I decided to stay. Going down the main staircase a bomb was dropped at the cross roads of Norfolk Street and Surrey Street. Standing in the doorway, we heard shouting, so we went outside to see. There

was the bomb crater, and the men around were saying they had to get to Crookes. We heard that Henry Hall and his band, who were playing at the Empire that week, had been in there when a bomb hit it, but we later learned that they were safe in the Grand Hotel. It was an awful experience listening to the explosions.

The all clear sounded about 4 o'clock, so I decided to go home. When I got to the top of Pinstone Street, it looked as if the Moor was on fire. No way was I going that way! So I went down Howard Street. Half way down was a deep crater and in the bottom of it was a car. You could hardly see, what with the smoke from the fires. When I got to the bottom of St Mary's Road, it was devastated. A mine had dropped there. I carried on until I got to Mappin & Webb's factory and thick smoke was coming across the road from Laver's. I eventually got to the top of East Bank Road when a bus came up and stopped to pick me up. What a night!

Sydney Middleton

Marion Stevens remembers

◀ Marion aged 20 and below, as she is today

◀ Marion Stevens (right) with her friend Jean Elsey

"I WAS in the Empire with my mother, hoping to see Henry Hall.

But, much to my disappointment, we were asked to leave when the sirens went. We were taken to a buidling nearby which made cardboard cartons but when it caught fire, we were moved elsewhere. As we sat and waited for the all-clear, watching families from round the town coming in from their bombed houses, I kept saying to mum 'Won't there be a long queue for a tram to get home!' We walked to the Wicker Arches, climbing over rubble and debris, finally arriving home in Shiregreen.

The first thing my father said was 'Where have you two been all night?'

I can't remember my mum's reply!"

Mrs M Stevens

Dorothy Oates remembers

"THE evening of the Sheffield Blitz I spent in the Don Picture Palace on West Bar.

I cannot remember the film I went to see but I have never forgotten what followed. I had my 17th birthday a couple of months before.

When we were allowed out after the all clear, there was such devastation.

Immediately opposite was the building everyone called The Relief (I suppose today it would be Social Security) which was flattened completely.

There was a tram on West Bar with the top deck completely sliced off.

As I walked home I saw other trams damaged, buildings reduced to rubble. Firefighters were still trying to put out the flames at Blanchards store on Infirmary Road. I didn't have much further to go as I lived near the Salvation Army meeting hall - but when I got there I found we had been bombed out.

◀ Dorothy right, in 1945

◀ Dorothy Oates in a dress made made from curtain material

No trams were running but that didn't mean we stayed home from work - we walked to town and at night I had to walk to Leppings Lane, to live with gran.

There was a wonderful feeling from one person to another at that time - I wish it was evident today."

Dorothy Oates

◀ Doroth Oates of Creswick St in a skirt made from black out material

▼ Dorothy as she is today

97

The Lord ▶ Mayor and Lady Mayoress talking to some of their guests at the Fleur de Lis service centre, Sheffield, where they entertained to lunch 40 members of the Forces from Sheffield convalescent homes. The party later visited the Union Street Picture Palace as guests of the management. The sign on the wall reminded them to keep off the beer!

During the war, beer was made slightly weaker, partly to try and combat an increase in drunken behaviour

DELUDE YOURSELF THAT BEER DOES YOU GOOD BECAUSE "IT DOESN'T"! ABSTAIN—SAVE

ALF TELLS US THAT ONE OF HIS AIR RAID PRECAUTIONS WAS CHANGING OVER TO DARK BEER, BECAUSE IT WAS INVISIBLE IN THE BLACK-OUT.

Alf's ARP Decision by Heap

Nellie Kenny remembers

"ON THE night of the Blitz, my niece and I went to the Hippodrome Cinema.

The big picture had just started when we went in and before long it was flashed on the screen there was an air raid so everyond had to get out. We were running along Pinstone Street when a policeman stopped us and told us to get to the

▲Nellie's niece Kathleen Entwistle

City Hall shelter. We had just got inside when a bomb dropped nearby. In

the shelter we met two soldiers who were stationed at Shirecliffe. We lived up Parkwood Springs so they said they would walk us home. When there was a lull we set off and had just got to West Bar when the bombs started again so we went into the shelter of the old men's hostel.

What struck me most was outside the hostel there were two tramcars, one was cut clean in half and the other was badly damaged and yet the drivers and conductors were in the shelter and hadn't a scratch on them.

We stayed there until the all clear and

▲ Nellie on her holiday in the Isle of Man

then set off home. We couldn't believe our eyes when we saw all the damage as we made our way to Neepsend.

As we walked up Birdwell Road to the railway arch, there was a big bang; it was a gas explosion over the very spot where we had walked. Believe me, we were four of the luckiest people to get out of town that night. "

Mrs N Kenny

◀ Nellie with a picture of herself when she was aged 18

◀ Nellie Kenny's wedding in 1942

Queen ▶ Elizabeth talks to Sheffield families bombed out of their homes and staying at a rest centre. Here Mrs Mary Elizabeth Rawlings and her baby meet the Queen

I'LL BE SEEING YOU!

10 Royal Guests

◀ *The Queen steps from the station for a tour of the bombed areas of Sheffield in January, 1941. The visit came about three weeks after the Blitz*

CIVIL Defence Commissioner for the North East, Lord Harlech rushed to Sheffield after the Blitz. He arrived in the still-smouldering city to pledge that everything possible would be done to get it back on its feet. He complimented the people of Sheffield with the words: "The people were tired in Sheffield, but on top of the job, well organised and getting down to it quickly." Another VIP visitor to the city in the immediate aftermath was General H R Alexander, later to become Lord Alexander of Tunis. He commented: "I was greatly struck by the cheerful-

The Royal visitors were shocked by what they saw...

ness and by the businesslike way in which everyone was tackling the job. It makes one feel very proud of our people to see how they stand up to such suffering."

It meant a great deal to the people of Sheffield to know that their suffering and resilience was valued and acknowledged.

That is why there was much excitement when the King and Queen paid a surprise visit to the city a few weeks after the raids.

King George VI's private secretary, Major A H L Harding told Lord Mayor, Ald Luther Milner: "The King has been distressed to learn of the damage done in Sheffield by the enemy's attacks and desires me to express his sincere sympathy with all who have suffered as a result of these raids. It is His Majesty's hope that he may be able to pay a visit to your city before long, and in the meantime he would be glad to know how matters are progressing."

In the ▶ company of the Lord Mayor of Sheffield, Ald Luther Milner, King George VI and Queen Elizabeth saw for themselves the terrible destruction of the Blitz on Britain's northern cities

The ▶ King and Queen at the community feeding centre at the City Hall, on January 6, 1942

Shortly after a progress report landed on the King's desk, his Royal Highness visited Sheffield accompanied by Queen Elizabeth, now the Queen Mother. They arrived on January 6, 1941 for a three hour stay, visiting bomb damaged homes, the new City Hall municipal restaurant and Firth Brown works. They also called in to offer words of comfort to those who had made their home at an emergency feeding centre in Anns Road Chapel, Heeley. Though not an official rest centre, this became a vital source of comfort and shelter for more than 300 people who had been made homeless by the bombing. The centre was immediately adopted by the Social Welfare Department of the city council which quickly supplied bunks and arranged for soldiers to do

They insisted on the car stopping to allow them to get out and walk around

the cooking in field kitchens set up in a school yard opposite. A team of WVS workers turned Anns Road into such an efficient centre that it was the last in the city to close. Its importance was underlined when the Royal couple paid a visit in January. (The centre was re-opened later in the war when 380 families evacuated from the south during attacks by the Germans' flying bombs, needed shelter.)

Twice, while being driven around the city, they insisted on the car stopping to allow them to get out and walk round damaged areas and talk with victims.

One woman called out to the King: "We shall get him," referring to Hitler. The King replied: "Yes, I think we shall."

At Firth Brown's the King borrowed the Chief Constable's sword to confer a knighthood, awarded in the New Year honours, on managing director Allan J Grant.

Around a week earlier, the Princess Royal and Lord Harewood had visited Sheffield to witness the bomb damage and to praise the people of Sheffield.

But though the Royal visitors were shocked by what they saw of Sheffield, they had not seen the worst. The clear up had got underway almost immediately and its effectiveness took even its organisers by surprise.

◀ The calm after the storm. A barrow filled with debris after cleaning up Blitz damage in Berkeley Road

In tribute ▶ to the key role played by Sheffield's industry towards the war effort, the Royal visitors made a point of calling in on the works which had been targeted by the Luftwaffe

Conditions on the post-Blitz roads were chaotic with 200 craters, broken tram wires, wrecked vehicles and seemingly endless debris.

But there was no time to stand around scratching heads. The clean up got underway at first light on the Friday morning, just three hours after the last bomber had returned to base. Squads of City Engineer Department workers, boosted by 200 men from the city council Parks Department, tackled the main roads and military routes first. Then they moved on to the less important roads.

By the end of the day, Sheffield could boast that buses were able to run on almost 30 suburban routes and normal service was resumed on 28 services outside the city boundary.

The buses used to carry out these duties may have looked sorry for themselves, battered and bomb-damaged as they were, but they were running and the city of Sheffield was back on the move, with a little help from Doncaster, Halifax, Huddersfield, Hull, Leeds, Newcastle, Todmorden and West Hartlepool, who all loaned vehicles to the city.

The tram network was more problematic. Tracks and miles of overhead wiring had been damaged and needed to be replaced. But even the trams were out and about by the weekend, running on undamaged stretches, notably from Norfolk Bridge to Tinsley, Attercliffe, Handsworth and Prince of Wales Road.

The Intake route was reopened on December 19 followed the next day by the Walkley and Crookes services. It was a similar story for Sheffield's well known high street stores which had been bombed out in the Blitz. They immediately began searching for alternative premises where they could hang up the Business As Usual signs.

The Grill Room of the Grand Hotel, the Cinema House and shops in Glossop Road, London Road, Ecclesall Road and West Street were taken over by Cockaynes, one of the leading names in city centre retailing. Similarly, Walsh's moved to The Mount, Broomhill while Marks and Spencer adapted the old Lansdown Cinema. British Home Stores moved into premises in Norfolk Street, Roberts Brothers found somewhere to set up shop in London Road and Ecclesall Road and the patched-up Central Picture House on The Moor was taken over by Atkinson's, who also found premises in the Telegraph Buildings, Cambridge Hall and Milton Hall. The Brightside and Carbrook Co-op took over the old Playhouse Theatre in Townhead Street.

The city council had kept 164 council homes empty since the start of the war in case they

were needed for people made homeless in the event of an air raid. Some of these were damaged in the raids but if they had survived, they would have been woefully inadequate.

The only answer to the huge problem facing Sheffield was to billet more than 36,000 people on other residents. That way shelter could be guaranteed for the homeless while work got underway making homes habitable. Great progress was made in this direction. But by the end of March, 1941, there were still 9,000 people in official billets.

◄ *More than 200 soldiers' wives, widows, old age pensioners and unemployed were given assisted price potato seeds, tools and fertilisers to encourage them to grow food on allotments*

" You must understand, Ethel, that the success of any campaign is largely dependent on the preliminary Staff Work."

◄ *Mary, Sally, Marie and Edith, the only gang of women railway platelayers in the North of England. The ages of the gang are 23, 25, 28 and 36. They and others like them helped keep transport going and aided a swifter return to a form of normality*

Pat ▶
Claxton
today

"I WAS only seven-years-old on the night of the Sheffield Blitz but my memory of that traumatic event is crystal clear.

We were sheltering on the cold stone cellar steps of 95, Shirebrook Road.

On the bottom step was my 23-year-old auntie Mary, crouching protectively over her two-year-old son, shielding him with her own body and one cushion, from the grit, soot and coal dust that filled our mouths and the debris that fell from the shaking walls, as wave after wave of bombers

thud. She did not stir from that position throughout the whole of that night.

Next up the flight of stone steps sat my 18-year-old auntie Ida, her warm arms

She sang in defiance all through that unforgettable night, rude songs about Hitler

firmly around me, keeping me safe within her embrace. She sang in defiance all through that unforgettable night - rude songs about Hitler, fighting songs and marching songs interspersed with "There'll Always Be An England" and "Land of Hope And Glory." Much later, the family said that her singing was worse than the bombing but, thinking that it was going to be our last night on earth, they let her get on with it.

At the top of the steps my mother was struggling with my gran, who was having hysterics, after being hit on the head by a very large, heavy bag of flour, that had been dislodged when the wooden cellar shelves and their contents descended on top of us.

The 10lb bag of

flour had burst on impact, showering us all with a film of white flour over our already sooty features.

We looked like a parody of the Black and White Minstrels.

▼*Auntie Ida sang rude songs about Hitler*

Auntie ▶
Mary
shielded
her son
with her
own body

dropped their deadly loads. Our old house creaked and groaned with each ear-splitting whistle and explosive

The only male present was my 26-year-old uncle George, who was awaiting further instructions from the Army. He was trying to open the cellar door to fetch a bottle of brandy to calm my gran's nerves, but the door had become firmly wedged to its frame.

Through the cellar grate we could see the orange glow and flickering flames from

▲ *Pat's mum, who was looking after gran*

the neighbouring houses that had received a direct hit, and there was the unmistakable smell of burning which I assume came from the doctor's house, which was well alight, and almost oppoosite our own home.

Three bombs had fallen on three sides of our property, all

Through the cellar grate we could see the orange glow and flickering flames

within 60 or 70 yards. When the all clear siren eventually came, our house was uninhabitable.

I feel very proud to have witnessed this period in my family's history, seeing and hearing for myself the extraordinary courage of just very ordinary people. They were a typical example of the rest of the British population during that stressful time. **99**

Pat Claxton

◀ *Uncle George tried to fetch a bottle of brandy*

◀ *Gran was hit on the head by a bag of flour*

◀ *Pat as a baby, sitting on the left*

The ► Blitz mass grave in City Road Cemetery. A hundred and thirty four victims are buried here. 'They died by enemy action'

IN THIS GARDEN
134 CITIZENS REST
IN A COMMUNAL
✠ GRAVE ✠
THEIR NAMES
ARE RECORDED
THEY DIED BY ENEMY ACTION
✠

This Christmas Eve message from the Lord Mayor and Lady Mayoress was published in The Star after the Blitz...

*D*URING the past days, we have spent every available minute in visiting all parts of the city, and in helping to make arrangements to relieve the sufferings of those in distress; for we were convinced that this was a time for 'Deeds not words'.

But on this day, the Eve of Christmas, we are prompted to pause for a few moments and address this message to you all.

To those who have suffered bereavement, we express our deepest sympathy. May you find comfort in the knowledge that the thoughts of your fellow citi-zens are with you in your dire distress.

To the injured, will you allow us to wish you a speedy return to good health.

To those who have lost their homes and also those who have had to leave them, we sincerely trust that in their temporary accommodation they have found understanding.

To those who, during the raid and since, have worked with unending energy, may we offer our warmest thanks.

And to all Sheffield citizens - may we express the hope that the spirit of Christmas will, in its noblest sense, inspire you with the tremendous courage needed to grapple successfully with the difficulties and trials that confront you.

Sheffield is still a city of proud and determined citizens!

Sheffield is your city and ours.

We beg of you, then, to join us in a firm resolve to carry on and to play our part until victory is achieved. Good Luck and God Bless You.

Luther F Milner, Lord Mayor, Lorna Milner, Lady Mayoress, December 1940.

◀ *Ald Milner*

◀ *Despite trauma and hardship, the people of Sheffield tried to make Christmas a happy one for the children*

THE ROLL OF HONOUR

THIS list, which pays tribute to the men, women and children who died in Sheffield during the Second World War, was compiled in the first instance by the Imperial War Graves Commission, who had this to say about the list.

"To a greater degree than before, the 1939-1945 war involved not merely armies, but entire nations.

The names of individuals mean little save to those who knew and loved them and mourn their loss, and the number of those who mourn will dwindle as the years pass by.

"But it is fitting that these names should be enrolled in Westminster Abbey, at the heart of the Commonwealth and among the most illustrious of the nation's dead, in commemoration of their suffering and as a tribute to their sacrifice."

ABBEY Ada Marion, age 77, of 422 Springvale Road, widow of William James Abbey. December 12 1940, at 422 Springvale Road.

ABBOTT Thomas Wilson, age 40, Home Guard. December 12 1940, at 103 Bloar Street.

ADDY Gertrude, age 56, of 9 Windsor Road, Heeley, wife of Joseph Addy. December 13 1940, at 9 Windsor Road.

ADDY Joseph, age 57, of 9 Windsor Road, Heeley, husband of Gertrude Addy. December 13 1940, at 9 Windsor Road.

ALCOCK Frederick, age 50, of 306 Queens Road, husband of Rose Alcock. December 13 1940, at 34 St Mary's Road.

ALLEN Mary Agnes, age 32, daughter of Mr J Allen of 235 Portobello Street. December 12 1940, at High Street.

ANTCLIFFE Arthur William, age 10, of 96 Bolsover Road, son of John William and Bella Antcliffe. December 15 1940, at 96 Bolsover Road.

ANTCLIFFE Bella, age 48, of 96 Bolsover Road, wife of John William Antcliffe. December 15 1940, at 96 Bolsover Road.

ANTCLIFFE Edith, age 13, of 96 Bolsover Road, daughter of John William and Bella Antcliffe. December 15 1940, at 96 Bolsover Road.

ANTCLIFFE John William, age 49, of 96 Bolsover Road, son of Maria Antcliffe, of 298 Barnsley Road, and of the late Hertbert Antcliffe, husband of Bella Antcliffe. December 15 1940, at 96, Bolsover Road.

APPLEBY John Thomas, age 60, Air Raid Warden, of 74 Phillimore Road, husband of Edith Appleby. December 15 1940, at ARP Post, Coleford Road.

ARMSTRONG Joseph, age 44, Air Raid Warden, of 56 Phillimore Road, husband of Leonora Armstrong. December 15 1940, at ARP Post, Coleford Road.

ARMSTRONG Leonora, age 41, Air Raid Warden, of 56 Phillimore Road, wife of Joseph Armstrong. December 15 1940, at ARP Post, Coleford Road.

ASHLEY William, age 46, of 11 Longley Close. March 14 1941, at Royal Hospital.

ATKIN Alan, age three, of 79 Oxford Street, grandson of the late Arthur and Elizabeth Atkin. December 13 1940, at 79 Oxford Street.

ATKIN Elizabeth, age 28, of 79 Oxford Street, daughter of the late Arthur and Elizabeth Atkin.

December 13 1940, at 79 Oxford Street.

ATKIN Elsie, age 36, of 79 Oxford Street, daughter of the late Arthur and Elizabeth Atkin. December 13 1940, at 79 Oxford Street.

ATKIN Frances, age 24, of 79 Oxford Street, daughter of the late Arthur and Elizabeth Atkin. December 13 1940, at 79 Oxford Street.

ASPINWALL Alfred, age 65, August 29 1940, at 25 St Stephen's Road.

AUCKLAND Annie Eliza, age 60, of 34 St Mary's Road. December 13 1940, at 34 St Mary's Road.

BAILEY Annie, age 37, of 70 Grove Street, wife of Arthur Bailey, December 13 1940, at 70 Grove Street.

BAILEY Arthur, age 41, of 70 Grove Street, husband of Annie Bailey, December 13 1940, at 70 Grove Street.

BARKER Albert, age 41, of 57 Titterton Street. December 15, 1940, at 11 Phillimore Road.

BARKWORTH Alfred, age 59, of 235 Hanover Street, husband of Maria Barkworth. December 12 1940, at 241 Hanover Street.

BARKWORTH Maria, age 59, of 235 Hanover Street, wife of Alfred Barkworth. December 12 1940, at 241 Hanover Street.

BARRATT Frederick Gordon, age 17, Home Guard, of 16 Gatefield Road, son of Edith Barratt, and of the late Samuel Frederick Barratt. Injured December 12 1940 at Sheffield, died December 14 1940, at Royal Hospital.

BARRATT Isaac, age 60, Home Guard, of 15 London Road, husband of Norah Barratt. December 12 1940 at 15 London Road.

BATTERSBY John William, age 53, ARP of 29 Stockton Street, Pitsmoor, husband of A E Battersby. December 12 1940, at 29 Stockton Street.

BATTLE Frank, age 61, of 78 Dobcroft Road. December 13 1940, at Abbeydale Road, Millhouses.

BAXTER Jane, age 77, of 201 Olive Grove Road, Heeley, wife of Lewis Baxter. December 12 1940, at 201 Olive Grove Road.

BAXTER Lewis, age 77, of 201 Olive Grove Road, Heeley, husband of Jane Baxter. December 12 1940, at 201 Olive Grove Road.

BEARD Annie, age 60, of 40 Joshua Road, wife of James

William Beard. December 12 1940, at 40 Joshua Road.

BEARD James William, age 62, of 40 Joshua Road, husband of Annie Beard. December 12 1940, at 40 Joshua Road.

BEARDSHAW Ethel, age 27, of 20 Fowler Terrace, daughter of James and Emma Dodd of 152 Cross Lane, Crookes, wife of Stanley Beardshaw. December 12 1940, at Marples Hotel, Fitzalan Square.

BEATSON Alice, age 41, daughter of Elizabeth Elshaw of 3 Hessle Street, wife of William Beatson of 2 Court, 5 House, Marshall Street. December 13 1940, at 3 Court, 4 House, Marshall Street.

BECK Ann Alice, age 65, of 58 Selborne Street, Attercliffe, wife of John Beck. December 15 1940, at 48 Selborne Street.

BECK George, age 34, ARP Ambulance Driver, husband of Florence Mabel Beck, of 28 Tapton Bank, Crosspool, December 13 1940, at Shoreham Street.

BECK John, age 67, of Selborne Street, Attercliffe, husband of Ann Alice Beck. Injured December 15 1940, at 48 Selbourne Street, died December 28 1940 at Royal Infirmary.

BENNETT Amy, age 69, of 274 Staniforth Road, widow of W Bennett. december 16 1940, at 272 Staniforth Road.

BERRISFORD Elsie Winifred, age 33, of 83 Southgrove Road, Ecclesall, daughter of Mrs Neil, of 6 Findon Street, wife of John Redfern Berrisford. December 13 1940, at Laurel Works, Nursery Street.

BERRISFORD John Redfern, age 33, of 83 Southgrove Road, Ecclesall, son of Mrs C Berrisford, of 38 Bradfield Road, husband of Elsie Winifred Berrisford. December 3 1940, at Laurel Works, Nursery St.

BIELBY Annie, age 45, of 74 Nether Edge Road, daughter of Susan and the late William Henry Bielby. December 12 1940 at 74 Nether Edge Road.

BIELBY Emily Hannah, age 51, MA of 74 Nether Edge Road, daughter of Susan and the late William Henry Bielby. December 12 1940, at 74 Nether Edge Road.

BIELBY Millicent Susan, age 54, of 74 Nether Edge Road, daughter of Susan and the late William Henry Bielby. December 12 1940, at 74 Nether Edge Road.

BIELBY Susan, age 84, of 74 Nether Edge Road, daughter of the late Mr and Mrs Sunley of Hartlepool, widow of William Henry Bielby. December 12 1940, at Royal Infirmary.

BIRD Thomas, 64, Air Raid warden, husband of Janet Bird, of 142 Cemetery Road, Sharrow, May 9 1941, at junction of Cemetery Road and Washington Road.

BIRTLES Kathleen, age 46, of 64 Bishopscourt Road, wife of Joseph Birtles. December 13 1940, at 64 Bishopscourt Road.

BIRTLES Peter, age 17, of 64 Bishopscourt Road, son of Joseph Birtles and of Kathleen Birtles. December 13 1940, at 64 Bishopscourt Road.

BIRTLES Sheila Mary, age 13, of 64 Bishopscourt Road, daughter of Joseph Birtles, and of Kathleen Birtles, December 13 1940, at 64 Bishopscourt Road.

BLAKEY George, age 27, of 370 Hollinsend Road, son of A and E Blakey, of 18 Reginald Street, husband of Alice Blakey. December 13 1940, at Farm Bank Road.

BLENKHORNE Emily Mary, age 68, of 92 Psalter Lane, wife of F W Blenkhorne. December 13 1940, at 92 Psalter Lane.

BLOOR Arthur William, age 18, of 117 Coleford Road. December 15 1940, at 117 Coleford Road.

BLOOR Harry, age 54, of 117 Coleford Road. December 15 1940. December 15 1940 at 117 Coleford Road.

BOARDMAN Clarence, age 31, of 56 Selbourne Street. December 15 1940, at 48 Selbourne Street.

BOARDMAN Hilary, age two, of 56 Selbourne Street, daughter of Clarence Boardman. December 15 1940, at 48 Selbourne Street.

BOOKER Albert William, age 77, of 21 Carfield Avenue, Meerbsrook, son of the late Coun Henry and Caroline Booker of Albert Road, Heeley, husband of the late Phoebe B Mallinson Booker. December 12 1940, at 21 Carfield Avenue.

BOOTH Dorothy, age 24, daughter of James Booth of 39 Cammell Road. December 13 1940, at 16 Daffodil Road, Firth Park.

BOOTH Rose Ann, age 41, of 49 Heather Road, wife of Harry Booth. December 13 1940, at 49 Heather Road.

BOTTOM Horace, age 44, of 16 Daffodil Road, Firth Park, son of Horace and Nellie Bottom, of 26 Coombe Road, Crookes; husband of Susie Bottom. December 13 1940 at 16 Daffodil Road.

BOTTOM Susie, age 49, of 16 Daffodil Road, Firth Park, wife of Horace Bottom. December 13 1940, at 16 Daffodil Road.

BOWER Clara Emily, age 62, of 3 Court, 1 House, Bangor Street, wife of Harry Bower. December 13 1940, at 3 Court, 1 House, Bangor Street.

BOWER Harry, age 63, of 3 Court, 1 House, Bangor Street, husband of Clara Emily Bower. December 13 1940, at 3 Court, 1 House, Bangor Street.

BRADLEY Emma, age 60, wife of Walter Bradley, of 133 Longley Avenue West, Shirecliffe Estate. December 13 1940, at Viaduct Inn, Wicker.

BREAN Annie, age 22, of 107 Pitsmoor Road, wife of F Brean. December 12 1940, at 107 Pitsmoor Road.

BREAR George William, age 56, of 116 St Mary's Road. December 13 1940, at 116 St Mary's Road.

BUSBY Charles William, age 60, of 4 Morley Street, Parkgate, Rawmarsh. August 19 1940 at Brinsworth Street.

BREEDON, George, age 11; of 9, Parkwood Road. Son of Cyril and Eva Mildred Breedon. 13 December 1940, at 9, Parkwood Road.

BREEDON, Terence, age 5 months; of 9, Parkwood Road. Son of Cyril and Eva Mildred Breedon. 13 December 1940, at 9 Parkwood Road.

BREEDON, Anita, age 3; of 9, Parkwood Road. Daughter of Cyril and Eva Mildred Breedon. 13 December, 1940, at 9, Parkwood Road.

BREEDON, Cyril, age 35; of 9, Parkwood Road. Son of Louisa Bingham (formerly Breedon), of 42, Lister Road; husband of Eva Mildred Breedon. 13 December, 1940, at 9, Parkwood Road.

BREEDON, Eva Mildred, age 32; of 9, Parkwood Road. Daughter of Louisa Walker, of 10, Fowler Terrace; wife of Cyril Breedon. 13 December, 1940, at 9, Parkwood Road.

BREWER, Arthur, age 33. Son of Earl and Mary Brewer, of 34, Thornhill Street, Savile Town, Dewsbury; husband fo Mary Brewer, of the same address. 12 December, 1940, at Marples Hotel, Fitzalan Square.

BRISBANE, Dorothy Ethel, age 42, of 43, Broomgrove Road. Wife of Robert Winning Brisbane. 12 December 1940, at Marples Hotel, Fitzalan Square.

BRISBANE, Robert Winning, age 40, of 43, Broomgrove Road. Husband of Dorothy Ethel Brisbane. 12 December 1940, at Marples Hotel, Fitzalan Square.

BROWN, Emily Jane, age 53; of 96, Cobden View Road. 22 December 1940 at Royal Hospital Annexe, Fulwood.

BROWN, Annie Amelia, age 42, of 18, Fleet Street. Daughter of Thomas and Annie Amelia Parkin; wife of Harry Brown. 15 December 1940, at 18, Fleet Street.

BROWN, Eric, age 12; of 18, Fleet Street. Son of Harry and Annie Amelia Brown. 15 December 1940, at 18, Fleet Street.

BROWN, Frank, age 10; of 18, Fleet Street. Son of Harry and Annie Amelia Brown. 15 December 1940, at 18, Fleet Street.

BROWN Harry, age 39, of 18 Fleet Street, husband of Annie Amelia Brown. December 15 1940, at 18 Fleet Street.

BROWN, Francis, age 70. Husband of Alice Ann Brown, of 86, Fairfax Road, Manor Estate. 12 December 1940, at Marples Hotel, Fitzalan Square.

BROWN Frederick, age 38, Air Raid Warden, of 71 Coleford Road, Darnall. December 15 1940, at ARP Post, Coleford Road.

BROWN Hilda, age 30, of 21 Bressingham Road, wife of George Brown. December 13 1940, at 21 Bresssingham Road.

BROWN John William, age 72, of 18 Perigree Road, husband of the late Mary Brown. December 13 1940, at 18 Perigree Road.

BROWN Muriel, age 32, of 18 Perigree Road, daughter of John William, and of the late Mary Brown. December 13 1940, at 18 Perigree Road.

BROWN Sydney Charles, age 49, of 9 Hackthorne Road. December 13 1940, at Shoreham Street.

BURGAN Mabel, age 30, of 183 Woodseats Road, wife of Arnold Stuart Burgan. December 13 1940, at 189 Woodseats Road.

BURGAN Stuart, age five, of 183 Woodseats Road, son of Arnold Stuart Burgan, and of Mabel Burgan. December 13 1940, at 189 Woodseats Road.

BURGESS Arthur Clarence, age 46, husband of Elsie Victoria Burgess, of 196 Bradway Road. December 12 1940, at Marples Hotel, Fitzalan Square.

BURGESS Emily Louisa, age 48, of 345 Springvale Road, wife of W F Burgess. February 4 1941 at 9 Slayleigh Avenue.

BURKINSHAW Albert, age 25, son of Mr J Burkinshaw, of 23 Haughton Road. December 12 1940, at Wilds, Lancing Road.

BURKINSHAW William, age 29, of 1 Hollindale Drive, husband of Ada Burkinshaw. December 13 1940, at 1 Queens Road.

BURT Olive, age 33, of 125 The Moor, wife of T C Burt. December 13 1940, at Porter Street shelter.

BUTCHER Alfred, age 49, husband of Nellie Butcher, of 15 Bernard Buildings. December 12 1940, at Marples Hotel, Fitzalan Square.

BUTLER Charles William, age 69, of 91 Bressingham Road. December 13 1940, at the Wicker.

BUTLER John Charles, age 33, Air Raid Warden, of 61 Tadcaster Road, Woodseats, husband of Eleanor Butler. December 12 1940, at Cross Burgess Street, died same day at Royal Hospital.

BUTLER Joseph William, age 41, husband of May Butler of 1 Harold Street, Walkley. December 13 1940, at 114 Heeley Bank Road.

BUTTERFIELD Alice Maria, age 63, of 63 Broomhall Street, wife of Frederick William Butterfield. December 12 1940, at 63 Broomhall Street.

BUTTERFIELD Frederick William, age 80, of 63 Broomhall Street, husband of Alice Maria Butterfield. December 12 1940, at 63 Broomhall Street.

BUXTON Ada, age 35, of 144 Sutherland Road, widow of T Buxton. December 12 1940, at Marples Hotel, Fitzalan Square.

CANNON Emily Jane, age 69, of 71 Croft Buildings, Campo Lane, widow of A W Cannon. December 12 1940, at 71 Croft Buildings.

CARBUTT Charlotte Cawthorne, age 56, of 63A Broomhall Street, daughter of the late John and Anne Ward, of Grimsby; wife of William Carbutt. December 12 1940, at 63A Broomhall Street.

CARBUTT William, age 59, of 63A Broomhall Street, son of the late Mr and Mrs John William Carbutt of Grimsby; husband of Charlotte Cawthorne Carbutt. December 12 1940, at 63A Broomhall Street.

CARPENTER George Frederick William, age 40, son of George Alfred Carpenter of Ormonde Gardens, Leigh-on-Sea, Essex; husband of Violet Iris Carpenter, of 58 Dovedale Avenue, Barkingside, Essex. December 12 1940, at Marples Hotel, Fitzalan Square.

CARR Evelyn, age 36, daughter of the late A and E Lawless, of Musselburgh, Midlothian; wife of Jack Leslie Carr, of 32 Southey Drive. December 12 1940, at Marples Hotel, Fitzalan Square.

CASTLETON Harry, age 68, husband of E Castleton of 13 Brunswick Street. December 13 1940, at 38 St Mary's Road.

CAWTON Barbara, age two, of 36 St Mary's Road, daughter of William Cawton, and of Rose Mary Cawton. December 13 1940, at 36 St Mary's Road.

CAWTON Rose Mary, age 29, of 36 St Mary's Road, daughter of William Henry and Mary Ellen Martin, of 49, Slinn Street, wife of William Cawton. December 13 1940, at 36 St Mary's Road.

CHARLES Edith, age 51, wife of Andrew Charles of 139 Broom Lane, Rotherham. December 12 1940, at Marples Hotel, Fitzalan Square.

CHURCH Robert Gordon, age 36, of 2 Montague Place, Baker Street, London W1. December 13 1940, at 34 St Mary's Road.

CLARKE Samuel Ernest, age 41, of 47 Southey Hill, husband of Hattie Clarke. March 14 1941, at 47 Southey Hill.

CLARKE Charlotte Emma, age 73, of 38 Charlotte Road, wife of John George Clarke. December 12 1940, at 38 Charlotte Road.

CLARKE John George, age 73, of 38 Charlotte Road, husband of Charlotte Emma Clarke. Injured December 12 1940, at 38 Charlotte Road, died December 14 1940, at City General Hospital

CLARKE Elsie, age 44, of 201 Olive Grove Road, Heeley, daughter of Lewis and Jane Baxter, wife of George Clarke. December 12 1940, at 201 Olive Grove Road.

CLARKE George, age 44, of 201 Olive Grove Road, Heeley, husband of Elsie Clarke. December 12 1940, at 201 Olive Grove Road.

CLARKE John James Burley, age 45, of 22 Parkwood Road, Neepsend, son of Lettice Agnes, and of the late Samuel Clarke. December 13 1940, at 9 Parkwood Road.

COCKAYNE Jess, age 43, husband of Ida Mary Cockayne, of 128 Westdale Lane, East Gedling, Nottinghamshire. December 12 1940, at Marples Hotel, Fitzalan Square.

COCKER Alfred Robert, age 48, of 99 Valley Road, husband of Florence Cocker. December 12 1940, at 99 Valley Road.

COCKER Florence, age 45, of 99 Valley Road, daughter of Edward A and Harriet Chandler, of 61 Hamilton Road, Wimbledon, Surrey, wife of Alfred Robert Cocker. December 12 1940, at 99 Valley Road.

COCKERILL Beatrice, age 55, of 126 Fitzalan Street, daughter of Mr E Cockerill. December 12 1940, at 126 Fitzalan Street.

COGGON Sarah Ann, age 84, of 111 Pitsmoor Road, widow of Alfred Coggon. December 12 1940, at 111 Pitsmoor Road.

COOK Doris Mary, age 41, of 195 Olive Grove Road, wife of William Cook. December 12 1940, at 195 Olive Grove Road.

COOK Graham Rimmington, age six, of 195 Olive Grove Road, son of William Cook, and Doris Mary Cook. December 12 1940, at 195 Olive Grove Road.

COOPER Andrew, age four, of 119 Rock Street, Pitsmoor, son of W Cooper (HM Forces) and of Linda May Cooper. December 12 1940, at Fox Street shelter.

COOPER George, age four, of 119 Rock Street, Pitsmoor, son of W Cooper (HM Forces) and of Linda May Cooper. December 12 1940, at Fox Street shelter.

COOPER Henry, age five, of 119 Rock Street, Pitsmoor, son of W Cooper (HM Forces). December 12 1940, at Fox Street shelter.

COOPER Arthur, age seven, of 119 Rock Street, Pitsmoor, son of W Cooper (HM Forces) and of Linda May Cooper. December 12 1940, at Fox Street shelter.

COOPER Linda May, age 26, of 119 Rock Street, Pitsmoor, daughter of John Henry, and of the late Grace Thurtle, wife of W Cooper (HM Forces). December 12 1940, at Fox Street shelter.

COOPER Barbara, age 11, of 62 Selborne Street, Attercliffe, daughter of Richard Cooper and of Margaret Cooper. December 15 1940, at 48 Selborne Street.

COOPER Ellen, age 87, of Archway Hospital, Highgate, London. December 17 1940, at Nether Edge Hospital.

COOPER Francis William Edward Horton, age 74, of 34 Gatefield Road. December 20 1940, at Royal Hospital Annexe Fulwood.

COOPER Gordon Richard, age nine, of 62 Selborne Street, Attercliffe, son of Richard Cooper and of Margaret Cooper. December 15 1940, at 48 Selborne Street.

COOPER Harold, age 46, DCM Sgt Home Guard, Air Raid Warden, of 19 Thorpe House Avenue, husband of Lil Cooper. December 12 1940, at Marples Hotel, Fitzalan Square.

COOPER Janet, age four, of 62 Selborne Street, Attercliffe, daughter of Richard Cooper and of Margaret Cooper. December 15 1940, 48 Selborne Street.

COOPER Margaret, age 37, of 62 Selborne Street, Attercliffe, daughter of F and J Colley of 39 Musgrove Road, Shirecliffe Estate, wife of Richard Cooper. December 15 1940, at 48 Selborne Street.

COOPER Maureen, age six, of 62 Selborne Street, Attercliffe, daughter of Richard Cooper, and of Margaret Cooper. December 15 1940, at 48 Selborne Street.

COOPER Robert Horace, age 37, Air Raid Warden, of 107 Coleford Road, son of Isabella Cooper of 69 Basford Street, Darnall, husband of A Cooper. December 15 1940, at ARP Post.

COUSINS Colin, age 31, of 56 Leigh Street, Attercliffe, son of Willie and Kate Cousins, of 21 Campbell Road, Carbrook; husband of Florence Cousins. December 15 1940, at 56 Leigh Street.

COUSINS Colin, age nine, of 56 Leigh Street, Attercliffe, son of Colin and Florence Cousins. December 15 1940, at 56 Leigh Street.

COUSINS Florence, age 33, of 56 Leigh Street, Attercliffe, daughter of Bertha Terry, of 45 Makin Road, Darnall; wife of Colin Cousins. Injured December 15 1940, at 56 Leigh Street; died December 16 1940, at City General Hospital.

COUSINS Norman, age four, of 56 Leigh Street, Attercliffe, son of Colin and Florence Cousins. December 15 1940, at 56 Leigh Street.

COSTALL David, age 48, of 14 Westbrook Bank. December 12 1940, at 14 Westbrook Bank.

COVERLEY Florence, age 30, wife of G R Coverley, of 53 Upwell Street. December 13 1940, at Laurel Works, Nursery Street.

COWLEY Mary Ann, age 59, of 289 Ellesmere Road, wife of William Cowley. October 12 1941, at 289 Ellesmere Road.

COWLEY William, age 58, of 289 Ellesmere Road, husband of Mary Ann Cowley, October 12 1941, at 289 Ellesmere Road.

COX Eleanor, age 25, of 48 Deerlands Avenue, wife of Fred Cox. December 12 1940, at 159 Rock Street.

COX Fred, age 26, of 48 Deerlands Avenue, husband of Eleanor Cox. December 12 1940, at 159 Rock Street.

COX Lucy, age 15, daughter of Mr C H W Cox of 364 Windmill Lane. December 12 1940, at 159 Rock Street.

CRANE David Young, age 41, of 242 Derbyshire Lane, husband of Winifred Crane. Injured December 12 1940, at 242 Derbyshire Lane, died December 19 1940, at Royal Hospital Annexe, Fulwood.

CROOKES Patricia Ann, age two months, of 98 Hurlfield Road, daughter of H and S A Crookes. December 19 1940 at 98 Hurlfield Road.

CROSBY Reuben, aged 67, of 75 Meadowhead Avenue, son of Benjamin and Harriet Emma Crosby, husband of the late Mary Edith Crosby. December 12 1940, at 75 Meadowhead Avenue.

CROSS Lawrence Raymond, aged 25, FAP member, son of Mr and Mrs Cross, of High Storrs Crescent, December 13 1940, at St Mary's Road.

CROWTHER Eric Vera, age 24, son of George Robert and Edith May Crowther, of 38 Harbord Road, Woodseats. December 15 1940, at Royal Hospital.

CROWTHER James Arthur, age 40, December 15 1940, at 81 Whixley Road.

CROWTHER Mary Shuttleworth, aged 35, of 107 Rushdale Road, Meersbrook, daughter of Maud

Mary, and of the late James Crowther. December 12 1940, at 107 Rushdale Road.

CROWTHER Maud, age 60, of 107 Rushdale Road, Meersbrook, daughter of the late Thomas F and A Jarvis, of Pitsmoor, wife of James Crowther. December 12 1940, at 107 Rushdale Road.

CRYAN James, age 74, of 27 Hurworth Road, injured August 29 1940; died October 3 1940, at Royal Infirmary.

DABILL Peter Cyril, age 17, son of Doris Deamer (formerly Dabill) of 102 Hangingater Road, and of the late Frank Dabill. December 12 1940, at 116 Shirebrook Road.

DALBY Winifred, age 35, wife of Alfred Dalby of 34 Southey Drive. December 12 1940, at Marples Hotel, Fitzalan Square.

DANIELS George Harry, age 18, of 37 Clarkehouse Road. December 13 1940, at Ecclesall Road.

DAVIES Frederick William, age 47, of 34 Springhouse Road, Crookesmoor. Injured December 12 1940, at G H Lawrance Ltd; died December 13 1940, at Royal Infirmary.

DAVIS Norman Plaxton, age 23, of 11 Court 1, Summer Street, Walkley, son of George Edwin Davis of 75 Lindsay Avenue; husband of Phyllis Davis. December 12 1940, at Marples Hotel, Fitzalan Square.

DAVIS Phyllis, age 23, of 11 Court 1, Summer Street, Walkley, daughter of Mr and Mrs S Smith of the same address; wife of Norman Plaxton Davis. December 12 1940, at Marples Hotel, Fitzalan Square.

DEAN Barbara Mary, age two, of 18 Daffodil Road, Firth Park, daughter of Harold Dean and of Vera Edith Dean. December 13 1940, at 18 Daffodil Road.

DEAN Elizabeth, age 76, of 18 Daffodil Road, Firth Park, widow of William Richard John Dean. December 13 1940, at 18 Daffodil Road.

DEAN Mabel, age 30, of 14 Kimberley Street, daughter of Mrs J Siddall, of 27 Roundall Street, Attercliffe. December 12 1940, at Marples Hotel, Fitzalan Square.

DEAN Vera Edith, age 34, of 18 Daffodil Road, Firth Park, wife of Harold Dean. December 13 1940, at 18 Daffodil Road.

DIAL Catherine Patience, age 56, of 122 St Mary's Road, wife of Ernest Dial. December 13 1940, at 122 St Mary's Road.

DICKINSON Emma, age 26, of 30 Uttley Street, Darnall, wife of John Edwin Dickinson. December 15 1940, at 30 Uttley Street.

DICKINSON Maureen, age five, of 30 Uttley Street, Darnall, daughter of John Edwin Dickinson, and of Emma Dickinson. Injured December 15 1940, at 30 Uttley Street,

died December 21 1940, at Royal Hospital Annexe, Fulwood.

DICKSON George Edward, age 53, Air Raid Warden of 357 Manor Oaks Road, Wybourn Estate, husband of Lillie Dickson. December 16 1940, at 29 Manor Oaks Road.

DIXON Henry George, age 50, of 12 Court, 3 House, Brunswick Road, husband of Edith Dixon. December 12 1942, at Nether Edge Hospital.

DIXON Frederick Charles Theodore, age 59, of 20 Barncliffe Road, husband of L B Dixon. December 12 1940, at Marples Hotel, Fitzalan Square.

(For **DIXON** Margaret Madge, see **LOCKLEY**, Margaret Madge).

DODD Roy, age 10, of 168 Shoreham Street, son of Walter and Violet Dodd. December 13 1940, at 168 Shoreham Street.

DODD Vernon, age four, of 168 Shoreham Street, son of Walter and Violet Dodd. December 13 1940, at 168 Shoreham Street.

DODD Violet, age 37, of 168 Shoreham Street, daughter of Tom and Sarah Ann Nutthall, wife of Walter Dodd. December 13 1940, at 168 Shoreham Street.

DODD Walter, age 38, Home Guard, of 168 Shoreham Street, son of Walter and Maud Dodd, of 19 Hollythorpe Rise, Norton Lees, husband Violet Dodd. December 13 1940, at 168 Shoreham Street.

DOWKER Muriel, age 14, daughter of Florence B Dowker, of 5 Windsor Road,Meersbrook, and the late Edward Dowker. December 13 1940, at 9 Windsor Road.

DOYLE Harry, age 56, Air Raid Warden of 4 Ventnor Place, husband of Catherine Louisa . December 13 1940, at South View Road.

DUCE George Alfred, age 51, husband of Harriet Duce, of 18 Wybourn House Road, Wybourn Estate. December 15 1940, at Woodhouse and Rixon Ltd, Bessemer Road.

DUNN Lois, age 30, of 159 Rock Street. December 12 1940, at 159 Rock Street.

DUNN Peter, age six, of 159 Rock Street, son of Lois Dunn. December 12 1940, at 159 Rock Street.

DURDEY Jack, age 34, of 32 Cockayne Place, Meersbrook, son of John and Nellie Durdey, of 23 Fox Lane, Frecheville, husband of Sarah Durdey. December 12 1940, at 32 Cockayne Place.

DURDEY Sarah, age 33, of 32 Cockayne Place, Meersbrook, daughter of James Allen Hewitt and Harriet Hewitt of 41 Nettleham Road, Woodseats, wife of Jack Durdey. December 12 1940, at 32 Cockayne Place.

DUTTON George, age 32, of 70 Grove Street. December 13 1940, at 70 Grove Street.

DYE William, age 27, of 169 Woodseats Road. December 13 1940, at 189 Woodseats Road.

EAMES Elizabeth, age 47, of Hermitage Inn, London Road, wife of Robert Eames. December 12 1940, at Sheffield.

EAMES Robert, age 47, of Hermitage Inn, London Road, husband of Elizabeth Eames. December 12 1940, at Sheffield.

EASON Bella, age 71, of 31 Bridport Road, Darnall, wife of James Eason. December 15 1940, at 31 Bridport Road.

EASON Vera, age 33, of 31 Bridport Road, Darnall, daughter of James Eason and of Bella Eason. December 15 1940, at 31 Bridport Road.

EBBATSON Winifred Margaret Victoria, age 39, of 327 Crookesmoor Road. December 12 1940, at Marples Hotel, Fitzalan Square.

ELLIOTT Norman, age 35, of 62 Cockshutt Drive. December 12 1940, at Union Street.

EVANS Lucy Margaret, age 44, daughter of Charles Fairfax Evans and Ann Evans, of 997 Abbeydale Road. Injured December 13 1940, at Sheffield, died same day at Royal Infirmary.

FAGAN Joseph, age 51, of 5 Sorby Street, husband of M Fagan. December 29 1940, at 15 Buckenham Road.

FIDLER William, age 38, of 109 Rushdale Road. December 12 1940, at 109 Rushdale Road.

FLEMING Dorothy Muriel, age 18, daughter of J W and A E Fleming, of 76 Macro Street, Pitsmoor. December 13 1940, at Grove Street.

FLETCHER Barbara, age 15, of 101 Aldison Road North, daughter of Mr W F Fletcher. December 12 1940, at 101 Aldison Road North.

FLETCHER James, age 34, of 51 Kent Road. December 12 1940, at Marples Hotel, Fitzalan Square.

FLETCHER Lily, age 32, wife of Henry Irving Fletcher of 361 Main Road, Darnall, December 12 1940, at Marples Hotel, Fitzalan Square.

FORD Ernest William, age 44, of 16 Station Road, Wallingford, Berkshire. December 12 1940, at Sheffield.

FORSTER Emily, age 50, wife of Thomas Frederick Forster, of 37 Ellesmere Road. Injured December 13 1940, at 60 Shepherd Street, died same day at Royal Infirmary.

FOSTER Rosina May, age 25, of 15 Northcote Avenue, wife of John Foster. December 13 1940, at 11 Northcote Avenue.

FOSTER Winifred Emily, age 23, of 9 Heathcote Road, daughter of Mrs A Hart, wife of A S Foster. Injured December 13 1940 at Sheffield, died December 26 1940 at Royal Infirmary.

FOX Elsie, age 50, of 38 Joshua Road, wife of Jack Fox.December 12 1940, at 38 Joshua Road.

FOX Jack, of 38 Joshua Road, husband of Elsie Fox. December 12 1940, at 38 Joshua Road.

FOX John William, age 35, of 240 Derbyshire Lane, husband of Lydia Fox. December 12 1940, at 240 Derbyshire Lane.

FOX Lydia, age 39, of 240 Derbyshire Lane, daughter of Harriet Smith, of 102 Alexandra Road, Heeley, wife of John William Fox. December 12 1940, at 240 Derbyshire Lane.

FURNISS Frederick, age 72, of 42 Phillimore Road, Darnall. December 16 1940, at City General Hospital.

GALLOP George Ernest William, age 26, son of George and Emily Gallop, of Westfield Bungalow, Carr, Maltby, Rotherham, husband of Doris Gallop, of Westfield Terrace, Bramley, Rotherham. September 26 1940, at Standard Steel Works, Sheffield Road.

GANNON Harold, age 42, fireman, NFS, son of the late Joseph and Susanna Gannon, husband of Hilda Gannon, of 39 Moss Street. April 25 1944, at Hastilar Road.

GARLICK Alfred, age 30, AFS, son of James William and Beatrice Garlick, of 20 Neill Road, Hunters Bar, husband of Betsy Garlick, of 7 Cockayne Place. Injured December 12 1940, at Archer Road, died December 14 1940, at Royal Hospital.

GASCOIGNE Cecilia, age 46, Air Raid Warden, of 148 Coleford Road, wife of John Thomas Gascoigne. December 15 1940, at ARP Post, Coleford Road.

GASCOIGNE John Thomas, age 50, Air Raid Warden, of 148 Coleford Road, husband of Cecilia Gascoigne. December 15 1940, ARP Post, Coleford Rd.

GILL Alice Edna, age 32, of 226 Brookhill. December 15 1940, at 226 Brookhill.

GLAVES George, age 45, ARP Rescue Service, husband of Sarah Ann Glaves, of 219 Chesterfield Road. December 12 1940, at Westbrook Bank.

GLOSSOP Doris, age 30, of 34 Charlotte Road, wife of J H Glossop. December 15 1940, at Charlotte Road.

GLOSSOP Jack, age six, of 34 Charlotte Road, son of J H and Doris GlossopDecember 15 1940, at 34 Charlotte Road.

GOOCH George Henry William, age 15, of 32 Loughborough Road, West Bridgford, Nottinghamshire, son of George Gooch. Injured May 9 1941 at 32 Loughborough Road, died May 16 1941, at Royal Hospital Annexe, Fulwood.

(For **GOOCH**, Charles George and others, see West Bridgford list)

GOODISON Florence Blanche, age 68, of 19 East Road, wife of George Henry Goodison. December 13 1940, at 19 East Road.

GOODISON George Henry, age 68, of 19 East Road, husband of Florence Blanche Goodison. December 13 1940, at 19 East Road.

GOODISON Phoebe, age 42, of 79 Heeley Bank Road, wife of William Howe Goodison. December 13 1940, at 19 East Road.

GOODISON William Howe, age 41, of 79 Heeley Bank Road, son of George Henry and Florence Blanche Goodison, of 19 East Road, husband of Phoebe Goodison. December 13 1940, at 19 East Road.

GOODRICH Clara Kathleen, age 50, of 49 Ashland Road. December 12 1940, at 174 Devonshire Street.

GOTHARD Sarah Ellen, age 61, of 121A Foxglove Road, daughter of the late George and Sarah Jane Gothard. Injured December 12 1940, at 121A Foxglove Road, died December 22 1940, at City General Hospital.

GOULD Ernest Patrick, age 67, of 71 Porter Street. December 13 1940, at Porter Street shelter.

GRAINGE Clifford Weatherhead, age 27, son of Willie and Lily Grainge, of 42 Denton Avenue, Roundhay, Leeds, husband of Elsie Grainge, of 137 Wrose Road, Shipley. December 13 1940, at St Mary's Road shelter.

GREAVES Percy, age 18, of 72 Watery street, son of Mr E Greaves, December 12 1940, at Clyde Works shelter.

GRANT, Madeleine Elaine, age 32, of 250, Brook Hill. Daughter of Mr and Mrs Fred Billan, of 335, London Road; wife of Sidney Claude Grant. December 12, 1940, at 250 Brook Hill.

GRANT, Robert Sidney, age 61; of 250, Brook Hill. Son of Sidney and Mary M Grant, of 115, Cromwell Road, Bristol; husband of Lydia Evelyn Grant. December 12, 1940, at 250 Brook Hill.

GRAY, Herbert, age 58; of 34A, Myrtle Road. December 14, 1940, at City General Hospital.

GREEN, Herbert, age 58; of 34A, Myrtle Road. December 14, 1940, at City General Hospital.

GREEN, Madge, age 24. Daughter of Joseph Henry and Ellen Elizabeth Green, of 10, Grimesthorpe Road. December 13, 1940, at Laurel Works, Nursery Street.

GREEN, Michael, age 66; of 57, Croft Buildings, Campo Lane. Son of the late Michael and Anne Green, December 12, 1940, at 57 Croft Buildings.

GREEN, Winifred, age 35. Wife of H Green, of 53, Atherton Road, December 13, 1940, at Angel Street.

GUESS, Edith Annie, age 29. Daughter of Mrs L Westby, of 54, Lound Road, Handsworth; wife of Albert Guess, of the same address. December 12, 1940, at Marples Hotel, Fitzalan Square.

GUMMER, Florence Owen, age 47; of 118, St Mary's Road. December 13, 1940, at 118, St Mary's Road.

GUMMER, Sybil Glover, age 60; of 118, St Mary's Road. December 13, 1940, at 118, St Mary's Road.

GUTTRIDGE, Ezra Shaw, age 36; ARP. Husband of PHM Guttridge, of 96, Town Street, Canklow. September 4, 1940, at Canklow Road.

GYTE, James William, age 70; of 24, Sandford Grove Road. December 13, 1940, at 24 Sandford Grove Road.

HALL, Eliza, aged 88; of Devonshire Street. December 12, 1940, at 172, Devonshire Street.

HALL, Frederick Wright, age 38; of 204 Savile Street; husband of Jane (Jennie) Hall. December 13, 1940, at Midland Railway Yard, Savile Street.

HALL Jane (Jennie) age 35; of 204, Savile Street. Daughter of Anne Taylor, of 1, Walling Road, Brightside, wife of Frederick Wright Hall. December 13, 1940, at Midland Railway Yard, Savile St.

HALL, John Charles, age 53; Air Raid Warden. Husband of Lily Elizabeth Hall, of 22, Draper Street, Grimesthorpe. January 15, 1943, at Grimesthorpe Road Wardens' Post.

HALL, Lawrence, age 38; of 146, Coleford Road. Husband of A Hall. December 15, 1940, at ARP Post, Coleford Road.

HALL, Muriel, age 29; of 210. Worthing Road. Daughter of Hayden and Amy Hall. September 11, 1940, at 210A, Worthing Road.

HALLAM, Winifred Gladys, age 15, of 117, Coleford Road. Daughter of Joseph Henry and Nellie Hallam. December 15, 1940, at 117, Coleford Road.

HALLATT, Valerie, age 4. Daughter of John William and Violet Hallatt, of 55, Ashbury Road. December 12, 1940, 105, Bloor Street.

HALLOWS, Clara, age 40; of 60, Shepherd Street. Daughter of the late Charles and Elizabeth Hallows. December 13, 1940, at 60, Shepherd Street.

HANDLEY, Norman, age 12; of 63, Greenhill Avenue. Son of Mr R Handley. December 13, 1940, at 63, Greenhill Avenue.

HANDOVER, Florence Irene, age 36; of 114, St Mary's Road. Daughter of Mrs Bale of Wisbech Road, Outwell, Cambridgeshire; wife of Pte. John Henry Handover, Royal Army Ordnance Corps (killed in same incident). December 13, 1940, at 114, St Mary's Road.,

113

HARKNESS, David Bryden, age 41; ARP (Works). Husband of Annie Harkness, of BOC House, Armer Street.Injured August 19, 1940, at Armer Street; died August 22, 1940, at Rotherham Hospital.

HARRISON, Minnie, age 65; of 114, St Mary's Road. Widow of W H Handover. December 13, 1940, at 114, St Mary's Road.

HARRISON, Annie, age 64; of 424, Springvale Road, Crookes. Wife of Richard Harrison. December 12, 1940, at 424, Springvale Road.

HARRISON, Richard, age 62; of 424, Springvale Road, Crookes. Husband of Annie Harrison.December 12, 1940, at 424, Springvale Road.

HARRISON, Richard Arthur, age 23; of 424, Springvale Rd, Crookes. Son of Richard and Annie Harrison. Husband of Ruth Harrison. December 12, 1940, at 424, Springvale Rd.

HARRISON, Robert, age 38; 424, Springvale Road, Crookes. Son of Richard and Annie Harrison. December 12, 1940, at 424, Springvale Road.,

HATCH, Henry, age 80; of 35, Wentworth Street. December 19, 1940, at Nether Edge Hospital.

HATTERSLEY, Henry, age 63; of 21 Cookson Close. December 12, 1940, at Marples Hotel, Fitzalan Square.

HAWKSWORTH Beatrice, age 26, daughter of Thomas William and Lily Hawksworth, of 88 Page Hall Road. December 12 1940, at 65 Ellesmere Rd.

HAWLEY Harry, age 30, of 274 Staniforth Road, husband of Ida Hawley. December 16 1940, at 272 Staniforth Road.

HAYWOOD Clara, age 63, of 46 Ringstead Crescent. December 13 1940, at 46 Ringsstead Crescent.

HAYWOOD Ellen, age 65, of 46 Ringstead Crescent. December 13 1940, at 46 Ringstead Crescent.

HAYWOOD Frank, age 59, of 46 Ringstead Crescent. December 13 1940, at 46 Ringstead Crescent.

HAYWOOD Lawrence, age 55, husband of Lily Haywood, of 49 Prince of Wales Road. December 13 1940, at Angel Street.

HEELEY Barbara, age 10, of 23 Bressingham Road, daughter of Percy and Doris Heeley. December 13 1940, at 23 Bressingham Road.

HEELEY Doris, age 32, of 23 Bressingham Road, wife of Percy Heeley. December 13 1940, at 23 Bressingham Road.

HEELEY Percy, age 38, of 23 Bressingham Road, husband of Doris Heeley. Injured December 13 1940, at 23 Bressingham Road, died December 15 1940, at City General Hospital.

HEMMINGFIELD Walter, age 54, Air Raid Warden, son of Walter and Mary Hemmingfield, of Whittington Moor, husband of Clara Hemmingfield, of 72 Phillimore Road. Injured December 15 1940, at Coleford Road, died December 16 1940, at City General Hospital.

HESSEY Arthur, age 39, of Laurel Works, Nursery Street, son of Arthur Ellis Hessey, and Fanny Hessey, of 25 Horner Road, Abbeydale, husband of Edith Hessey. December 13 1940 at Laurel Works, Nursery Street.

HESSEY Edith, age 38, of Laurel Works, Nursery Street, wife of Arthur Hessey. December 13 1940, at Laurel Works, Nursery Street.

HILL Annie May, age 54, of 995 Abbeydale Road. December 13 1940, at 995 Abbeydale Road.

HILL Doreen Mary, age 10, of 77 Whixley Road, Darnall, daughter of Gnr Thomas Arthur Hill RA and Lucy Hannah Hill. December 15 1940, at 77 Whixley Road.

HILL Dorothy, age 27, of 222 Oxford Street, daughter of T A and Ethel Hill. December 13 1940, at 222 Oxford Street.

HILL Frederick William, age six, off 77 Whixley Road, Darnall, son of Gnr Thomas Arthur Hill RA and Lucy Hannah Hill. December 15 1940, at 77 Whixley Road.

HILL Jessie, age 15, daughter of Robert and Millicent Hill, of 18 Guilthwaite Crescent, Whiston. December 12 1940, at Ellesmere Road.

HILL, John Arthur, age 12; of 77, Whixley Road, Darnall. Son of Gnr. Thomas Arthur Hill, RA, and Lucy Hannah Hill. December 14, 1940, at 77, Whixley Road.

HILL, Lucy Hannah, age 34; of 77, Whixley Road, Darnall. Daughter of Ethel Stevens (formerly Ogle), of 7, Guest Road, and of the late Benjamin Ogle; wife of Gnr. Thomas Arthur Hill, RA (killed in the same incident). December 14, 1940, at 77, Whixley Road.

HILL, Nellie, aged 49, of 2, Court, 5, Kilton Street. Wife of Frank Hill. December 13, 19450, at 2, Court, 5, Kilton Street.

HODSON, Elizabeth, age 76; of 116, St Mary's Road. Wife of John Hodson. December 13, 1940, at 116, St Mary's Road.

HODSON, John, aged 73; of 116, St Mary's Road. Husband of Elizabeth Hodson. December 13, 1940, at 116, St Mary's Road.

HOGGINS, Henry John, age 30; of 3, West Street, Lower Gornal; Staffordshire. Husband of Adelaide Agnes Hoggins. December 12, 1940, at Marples Hotel, Fitzalan Square.

HOLLAND, Kate, age 60; of Crofts Buildings, Campo Lane. December 12, 1940, at Crofts Buildings.

HOLMES, Samuel, age 48; of 160 Fox Street. Husband of Emma Holmes. December 12 1940, at 60 Fox Street.

HOMER, Joyce, age 21; of 52, Kenwood Park Road. December 13, 1940, at 52, Kenwood Park Road.

HOWARD, Edward Henry, age 62. Husband of Nellie Howard, of 264, Coleford Road, Darnall. December 12, 1940, at Sheffield.

HOWE, Grace Winifred, age 38; of 127, Lancing Road. December 12, 1940, at 127, Lancing Road.

HOWSON, Arnold, age 34. Son of Arthur and Martha Howson, of 3, Court 1, House, Napier Street; husband of Mary Howson, of 15, Coombe Road, Crookes. December 12, 1940, at Craven Works shelter, Darnall.

HUKIN, Thomas, age 49; of 86, Huntingtower Road, Ecclesall. Husband of the late Edith Hukin. December 13, 1940, at Ecclesall Road.

HULLEY, Elsie, age 39; of 243, Hanover Street. Wife of Reginald John Hulley. December 12, 1940, at 243, Hanover Street.

HULLEY, Gerald, age 13; of 243, Hanover Street. Son of Reginald John and Elsie Hulley. December 12, 1940, at 243, Hanover Street.

HULLEY, Herbert Cyril, age 44. Husband of Anne D. Hulley, of 19, Langdon Street, Sharrow. December 13, 1940, at Earl Street shelter.

HULLEY, Reginald John, age 43; of 243, Hanover Street. Husband of Elsie Hulley. December 12, 1940, at 243, Hanover Street.

HUNTER, Charles Edward, age 18; of 20, William Street. Son of Charles Hunter, and of the late Eliza Hunter. December 12, 1940, at Nether Edge Hospital.

HUNTER, George James, age 72; of 197, Darnall Road, Darnall. December 15, 1940, at 197, Darnall Road.

HURT, Harry, age 44; of 22, Fleet Street, Newhall. December 15, 1940, at 18, Fleet Street.

HURT, Mary (Polly) age 48; of 22, Fleet Street, Newhall. December 15, 1940, at 18, Fleet Street.

HUTCHINSON, Barrie, age 5 months; of 25, Bressingham Road. Son of Samuel Douglas and Mary Ellen Hutchinson. December 13, 1940, at 25 Bressingham Road.

HUTCHINSON, Patricia, age 8; of 25, Bressingham Road. Daughter of Samuel Douglas and Mary Ellen Hutchinson. Injured December 13, 1940, at 25, Bressingham Road; died same day at City General Hospital.

IBBOTSON, Winifred Grace, age 29; of 62, Bishopscourt Road, Norton Lees. Daughter of Minnie Long, of 10, Harcourt Crescent, Crookesmoor, and of the late Frederick Hughes Long; widow of Francis F. Ibbotson. December 13, 1940, at 62, Bishopscourt Road.

JACKLIN, Lucy Helen, age 73; of 19, East Road. Widow of R R Jacklin., December 13, 1940, at 19, East Road.

JACKSON, Annie Ellen, age 59; of 322, Brightside Lane. Wife of John Jackson. Injured December 13, 1940, at junction of Brightside Lane and Alfred Road; died same day at City General Hospital.

JACKSON, Ellen, age 58; of 72, Grove Street. Wife of Robert William Jackson. December 13, 1940, at 70, Grove Street.

JACKSON, Frederick, age 64. Husband of Emily Jackson, of 8, Ratcliffe Road. December 12, 1940, at Collegiate Crescent.

JACKSON, Robert William, age 59; of 72, Grove Street. Husband of Ellen Jackson. December 13, 1940, at 70, Grove Street.

JACKSON, Frederick, age 64. Husband of Emily Jackson, of 8, Ratcliffe Road. December 12, 1940, at Collegiate Crescent.

JACKSON, Robert William, age 59; of 72, Grove Street. Husband of Ellen Jackson. December 13, 1940, at 70, Grove Street.

JACKSON, William, age 56. Husband of Ada Jackson, of 15, Robertshaw Street. December 12, 1940, at Corporation Flats, Campo Lane.

JARVIS, Elias, age 28. Son of Mr W Jarvis, of 77, Yew Lane, Ecclesfield. December 12, 1940, at 65, Ellesmere Road.

JARVIS, Thomas Alfred, age 55; of 107, Rushdale Road, Meersbrook. Son of the late Thoms F and Mary A Jarvis. Injured December 12, 1940, at 107, Rushdale Road; died December 16, 1940, at Royal Hospital.

JEFFERSON, John, age 37; Home Guard; of 5 Hollythorpe Road, Norton Lees. Son of Joseph and Alice Jefferson, of 36, Pearson Place, Meersbrook; husband of Marjorie Jefferson. December 12, 1940, at Wilds, Lancing Road.

JENKINSON, Arthur, age 61; of 358, Gleadless Road, Heeley. Son of the late Fernel and Hannah Jenkinson, of 228, Warminster Road; husband of Beatrice Annie Jenkinson. December 12, 1940, at 358, Gleadless Rd.

JEPSON, Elise Mary, age 29; of 157, Rock Street. Daughter of Mrs M E Churchill, of 224, Marcus Street, Pitsmoor; wife of J S Jepson. December 12, 1940, at 157 Rock Street.

JERVIS, Philip, age 35. Husband of Harriet Jervis, of 270, Prince of Wales Road. Injured December 12, 1940, at 270, Prince of Wales Road; died December 13, 1940, at Royal Hospital.

JOHNSON, Barbara, age 2; of 16, Perigree Road. Daughter of L/Cpl H Johnson, The York and Lancaster Regiment, and of Gladys Johnson. December 12, 1940, at 16 Perigree Road.

JOHNSON, Dennis, age 4; of 16, Perigree Road. Son of L/Cpl H Johnson, The York and Lancaster Regiment, and of Gladys Johnson. December 13, 1940, at 16, Perigree Road.

JOHNSON, Ethel, age 51; of 194, Western Road. December 14, 1940, at Royal Hospital Annexe, Fulwood.

JOHNSON, Gladys, age 28; of 16, Perigree Road. Wife of L/Cpl H. Johnson, The York and Lancaster Regiment. December 13, 1940, at 16 Perigree Road.

JOHNSON, John Arthur, age 66; of 47, Bridport Road, Darnall. Injured December 15, 1940, at 47, Bridport Road; died December 18, 1940, at City General Hospital.

JOHNSON, Margaret, age 16 months; of 16, Perigree Road. Daughter of L/Cpl H Johnson, The York and Lancaster Regiment and of Gladys Johnson. December 13, 1940, at 16, Perigree Road.

JONES, Ann Eliza, age 84, of 69, Cottingham Street. Deecember 15, 1940, at 69, Cottingham Street.

JONES, Douglas Richards, age 23, of 123, Hammond Street. Son of Aldred Sydney and Phoebe Jones of 9, Horam Road, Crookesmoor Road. Injured August 29, 1940, at 123, Hammond Street, died same day at Royal Infirmary.

JONES, Joseph Bullons, age 62. Husband of Emma Jones, of 353, Sharrow Vale Road. December 12, 1940, at Hermitage Inn, London Road.

JONES, Marjorie, age 28. Daughter of Oscar and Helen Mary Jones, of 58, Wake Road. December 13, 1940, at Porter Street Shelter.

KENDELL, Nora, age 23; of 20, Belper Road. Wife of Dennis Kendell. December 13, 1940, at Laurel Works, Nursery Street.

KENNY, Sylvester, age 47; of 199, Musgrave Crescent. Husband of Alice Kenny. December 12, 1940, at Musgrave Crescent.

KENNY, William, age 14; of Musgrave Crescent. Son of Alice Kenny, and of Sylvester Kenny. December 12, 1940, at Musgrave Crescent.

KENTON, James, age 67; of 71, Havelock Square. Husband of Sarah Ellen Kenton. December 13, 1940, at 71, Havelock Sq.

(For **KENTON,** Sarah Ellen, see Wortley list).

KHAN, Edna May Ahmed, age 22. Daughter of Flora Marshall, of 11, Wilkinson Street; wife of Ali Ahmed Khan, of 11A Filey Street,. December 12, 1940, at Marples Hotel, Fitzalan Sq.

KING, Margaret, age 64; of 189, Woodseats Road. Widow of Arthur William King. December 13, 1940, at 189, Woodseats Rd.

KING, Thomas Michael, age 18

months; of 189, Woodseats Road. Son of Bertha King and of Thomas P King. December 13, 1940 at 189, Woodseats Road.

KING, Thomas P., age 27; of 189, Woodseats Road. Son of Margaret, and of the late Arthur William King; husband of Bertha King. December 12, 1940, at 189, Woodseats Road.

(for **KING,** Bertha, see Warrington R.D. list).

KING, Tom, age 33. Husband of Lilian Ida King, of 17, Saunders Road, Wybourn. December 16, 1940, at 17, Saunders Rd.

KIRBY, William, age 57. Husband of Elizabeth Kirby, of 99, Dagnam Road. December 12, 1940, at Marples Hotel, Fitzalan Sq.

LANGSTAFF, Mary Ann, age 73; of 116, Shirebrook Road, Heeley. December 12, 1940, at 116, Shirebrook Road.

LARGE, Donald McLeod, age 29; of Lynwood, Coed Coch, Old Colwyn, Denbigh, Wales. December 13, 1940, at 38, St Mary's Road.

LATHAM, Harry, age 41. Husband of Alice Latham, of 98, Devonshire Road, Bolton, Lancashire. December 13, 1940, at Porter Street Shelter.

LAWRENCE, George Herbert, age 52. Husband of Elsie Lawrence, of Belmont, Hathersage, Derbyshire. December 13, 1940, at Laurel Works, Nursery Street.

LAYCOCK, Harriet Susan, age 60; of 20, Fleet Street, Brightside Lane. Daughter of the late Thomas Allen Payne, and Emma Payne, of 95, Freedom Street; widow of Lawrence Laycock. December 15, 1940, at 18, Fleet Street.

LAYCOCK, Thomas Leslie, age 30; of 20, Fleet Street, Brightside Lane. Son of Harriet Susan, and of the late Lawrence Laycock. December 15, 1940, at 18, Fleet Street.

LECLERE, Doris, age 13; of 79, Queen's Road, Gosport, Hampshire. Daughter of Mr E Leclere. December 12, 1940, at 174 Devonshire Street.

LECLERE, Eileen, age 10, of 79, Queen's Road, Gosport Hampshire. Daughter of Mr E Leclere. December 12, 1940, at 174 Devonshire Street.

LECLERE, Lily, age 66; of 174, Devonshire Street. December 12, 1940, at 174, Devonshire Street.

LEE, Patricia, age 3, of 73, Fowler Street, Pitsmoor. Daughter of Bernard and Kathleen Lee. December 13, 1940, at 70 Grove St.

LEE, Sebra Ann, age 60; of 75, Whixley Road. Widow of W Lee, December 14, 1940, at 75, Whixley Road.

LEESLEY, John, age 56; of 1, Beeton Road, Meersbrook. Son of the late John and Elizabeth Leesley, of 46, Burcot Road, Meersbrook. December 12, 1940,

at Hermitage Inn, London Rd.

LEEVERS, Cyril, age 20. Son of Alfred and Frances A Leevers, of 68, Holmhirst Road, Woodseats. December 12, 1940, at Wilds, Lancing Road.

LEYLAND, Agnes Maud, age 55; of 34, St Mary's Road. Widow of Thomas Leyland. Injured December 13, 1940, at 34, St Mary's Road; died December 15, 1940, at Royal Hospital.

LILLEY, Clara, age 77; of 45, Steade Road. December 12, 1940, at 45, Steade Road.

LISHMAN, Kenneth, age 16; of 33, Jessell Street. December 13, 1940, at Porter Street Shelter.

LOCK Frances Kate, age 52, of 195 Olive Grove Road, Heeley, wife of Ernest James Lock. December 12 1940, at 195 Olive Grove Road.

LOCKWOOD Joseph, age 70, of 51 Broomhall Street, husband of Agnes Lockwood. December 12 1940, at 51 Broomhall Sreet.

LODGE Catherine Helen, age four months, of 59 Westbourne Road, daughter of John David Lodge, and of Leone Marie Clementine Lodge. December 12 1940, at 59 Westbourne Road.

LODGE Harry, age 64, of 59 Westbourne Road, husband of Violet Isobel Lodge. December 12 1940, at 59 Westbourne Road.

LODGE Leone Marie Clementine, age 23, of 59 Westbourne Road, wife of John David Lodge. December 12 1940, at 59 Westbourne Road.

LONGDEN Florence, age 25, of 212 London Road, daughter of Arthur Wathall, of 7 Yarborough Road, Abbeydale, wife of Gnr C Longden RA. December 12 1940, at Marples Hotel, Fitzalan Square.

LONKES Edith, age 67, of 197 Olive Grove Road, Heeley, wife of Joseph William Lonkes. December 12 1940, at 197 Olive Grove Road.

LONKES Joseph William, age 68, of 197 Olive Grove Road, Heeley, husband of Edith Lonkes. December 12 1940, at 197 Olive Grove Rd.

LUMB Percy, age 53, husband of C Lumb of 47 Barber Road. December 12 1940, at Sheffield.

MacBETH George, age 37, Second/Lieut Home Guard, of 7 Southbourne Road, husband of Amelia Morton Mary MacBeth. October 20 1941, at 7 Endcliffe Terrace Road.

McGILVRAY William Andrew, age 68, of 4 Oatlands Drive, Newall, Otley. December 13 1940, at 548 Ecclesall Road.

MACHEN Wilfred, age 18, of 13 Exeter Street, son of Wilfred Ernest Machen. December 12 1940, at 17 Exeter Street.

MACHEN Wilfred Ernest, age 51, of 13 Exeter Street, December 12 1940, at 17 Exeter Street.

MACIOCE Joan, age nine, of 113

Meadow Street, daughter of Joseph Macioce. December 13 1940, at 113 Meadow St.

MACIOCE Joseph, age 42, of 113 Meadow Street. December 13 1940, at 113 Meadow Street.

McLARDY James, age 60, of 20 Sedan Street, Pitsmoor, husband of A L McLardy. December 12 1940, at 65 Ellesmere Road.

McLEAN Hugh, age 62, of 115 Rushdale Road, son of Charles and Eliza McLean of 25 Walkden Road, Walkden, Manchester, husband of Louisa McLean. December 13 1940, at 115 Rushdale Road.

MAKIN Betty, age 17, of 41 Southey Hill, Parson Cross, daughter of Peter and Doris Makin. March 14 1941 at 41 Southey Hill.

MAKIN Doris, age 43, of 41 Southey Hill, Parson Cross, daughter of Mr and Mrs Coles, of 566 Boston Street, wife of Peter Makin. March 14 1941, at 41 Southey Hill.

MAKIN Jean, age nine of 41 Southey Hill, Parson Cross, daughter of Peter and Doris Makin. March 14 1941, at 41 Southey Hill.

MAKIN Peter, age 45, of 41 Southey Hill, Parson Cross, son of Mr and Mrs Makin of View Road, husband of Doris Makin. March 14, 1941 at 41 Southey Hill.

MAKIN Roy, age 14, of 41 Southey Hill, Parson Cross, son of Peter and Doris Makin. March 14 1941, at Southey Hill.

MALLAM Frederick, age 80, of 174 Devonshire Street, December 12 1940, at 174 Devonshire St.

MALLINSON Joseph Wycliffe, age 48, of 55 Broomhall Street, husband of Winifred Mary Mallinson. December 12 1940, at 55 Broomhall Street.

MARKINSON Eunice, age 23, daughter of Mrs M Markinson, of 25 Guilthwaite Crescent, Whiston, Rotherham. December 13 1940, at Porter Street shelter.

MARSDEN, Florence, age 25, of 38, Barrack Lane, wife of A Marsden. December 12, 1940, at 38, Barrack Lane.

MARSDEN, Joseph Clifford, age 66, of 16, Machon Bank Road. December 12, 1940, at Marples Hotel, Fitzalan Square.

MARSHALL, Gordon Edward, age 10, of 107, Bloor Street, Walkley, son of Edward Marshall, and of Sarah Ann Marshall. Injured December 12, 1940, at 197, Bloor Street, died December 13, 1940, at Royal Infirmary.

MARSHALL, Sarah Ann, age 37, of 107, Bloor Street, Walkley, daughter of Thomas and Sarah Ann Fox, of 13, Wordsworth Close, Parson Cross, wife of Edward Marshall, injured December 12, 1940, at 107, Bloor Street, died December 13, 1940, at Royal Infirmary.

MARSHALL, Terence, age 5, of 107, Bloor Street, Walkley, son of Edward Marshall, and of Sarah Ann Marshall, injured December 12, 1940, at 107, Bloor Street, died December 13, 1940, at Royal Infirmary.

MARSHALL, William Frederick Wilfred, age 67; of 94, Montgomery Road. February 25, 1951, at 9, Williamson Road.

MASON, James, age 17. Home Guard. Son of James Arthur and Harriet Emma Mason, of 83, Idsworth Road, Firth Park. December 13, 1940, at Porter Street Shelter.

MATTHEWMAN, Sylvia, aged 18, of 14, Thirlmere Road, Abbeydale. Daughter of Horace Matthewman, of Selwyn House, Brampton Bierlow, Rotherham. December 14, 1940, at St Mary's Road.

MEADOWS, George William, age 58, of 52, Sandford Grove Road. Husband of Martha Wilhelmina Meadows. December 13, 1940, at 52, Sandford Grove Road.

MERCER, John Thomas, age 5, of 29, Burnt Tree Lane. Son of Leonard and Winifred Jane Mercer. December 13, 1940, at 29, Burnt Tree Lane.

MERCER, Leonard, age 33, of 29, Burnt Tree Lane . Son of Mr and Mrs John Mercer, husband of Winifred Jane Mercer. December 13, 1940, at 29, Burnt Tree Lane.

MERCER, Pauline, age 3, of 29, Burnt Tree Lane. Daughter of Leonard and Winifred Jane Mercer. December 13, 1940, at 29, Burnt Tree Lane.

MERCER, Peter, age 2, of 29, Burnt Tree Lane. Son of Leonard and Winifred Jane Mercer. December 13, 1940, at 29, Burnt Tree Lane.

MERCER, Winifred Jane, age 28, of 29, Burnt Tree Lane. Daughter of Thomas and Ada Tutin of 37, Briar Street, Nottingham, wife of Leonard Mercer. Injured December 13, 1940, at 29, Burnt Tree Lane, died same day at Royal Infirmary.

MIDDLETON, Annie, age 37, of 285, Ellesmere Road. Daughter of Daniel and Harriet A Hooper, of 291, Ellesmere Road, wife of Horace Middleton. Injured October 12, 1941, at 285 Ellesmere Road, died October 14, 1941, at Royal Infirmary.

MIDDLETON, Arnold, age 51, of 19, Exeter Road. December 12, 1940, at 19, Exeter Road.

MIDDLETON, David Robert Bruce, age 68, of 15, Chatfield Road, Woodseats. December 13, 1940, at Porter Street Shelter.

MIDDLETON, Horace, age 40, of 285, Ellesmere Road. Husband of Annie Middleton. Injured October 12, 1941, at 285, Ellesmere Road, died October 19, 1941, at Royal Infirmary.

MIDDLETON, Joan, age 8, of 285, Ellesmere Road. Daughter of Horace and Annie Middleton. October 12, 1941, of 285,

Ellesmere Road.

MIDDLETON, John Siddall, age 53, of 13, Court, 5 House, Woodside Lane. Son of Mary Middleton. December 12, 1940, at 11 Court, 3 House, Woodside Le.

MIDDLETON, Mary, age 86, of 11, Court, 3 House, Woodside Lane. December 12, 1940, at 11 Court, 3 House, Woodside Lane.

MILLS, John Walter, age 54, of 115, Archdale Road. December 12, 1940, at 115, Archdale Road.,

MILNER, Margaret, age 50, of 41 Grove Street. Wife of E. Milner. December 13, 1940, at 66 Grove Street.

MILNER, Mary Teresa, 12, of 41, Grove Street. Daughter of E. Milner and of Margaret Milner. December 13, 1940, at 66 Grove Street.

MILTON, Alice, age 58, of Woodseats Road. Widow of William Milton. December 13, 1940, at 140 Woodseats Road.

MINOTT, Alfred Vincent, age 19, of 15, London Road. Son of Alfred Minott, and of Beatrice May Minott. December 12, 1940, at 15, London Road.

MINOTT, Beatrice May, age 41, of 15, London Road. Daughter of Harry and Sarah Low, wife of Alfred Minott. December 12, 1940, at 15, London Road.

MINOTT, Margaret Shirley, age 12, of 15, London Road. Daughter of Alfred Minott, and of Beatrice May Minott. December 12, 1940, at 15 London Road.

MITCHELL, Agnes, age 54, of 107, Pitsmoor Road. Wife of A Mitchell. December 12, 1940, at 107, Pitsmoor Road.

MITCHELL, Archie, age 14, of 107, Pitsmoor Road. Son of A Mitchell, and of Agnes Mitchell. December 12, 1940, at 107, Pitsmoor Road.

MITCHELL, Gordon, age 12, of 107, Pitsmoor Road. Son of A Mitchell and of Agnes Mitchell, December 12, 1940, at 107, Pitsmoor Road.

MITCHELL, Violet, age 18, of 107, Pitsmoor Road. Daughter of A Mitchell, and of Agnes Mitchell. December 12, 1940, at 107, Pitsmoor Road.

MOFFATT, Oliver Robert, age 41, of Green Bank, Manchester Road, Burnley. December 13, 1940, at Porter Street Shelter.

MONKS, Alice, age 41. Daughter of Emma Mills, of 35, Harvest Lane, and of the late George Mills, wife of Thomas Monks of 15, Warley Road. Manor Lane. September 26, 1940, at 15, Warley Road.

MOORE, Arthur, age 28; Driver, AFS. Son of Arthur Harrison Moore and Elizabeth Fanny Moore, of 7, Arnside Road. December 13, 1940, at Burgess Street.

MOORHOUSE, Ernest, age 42; of 29, Bute Street, December 16,

1940, at Nether Edge Hospital.

MORLEY, Mary, age 76; of 64, Cottinghanm Street, Attercliffe. Widow of W H Morley, December 15, 1940, at 64 Cottingham St.

MORRIS, Joseph, age 58; ARP Rescue Service of 186, Holme Lane. December 12, 1940, at Marples Hotel, Fitzalan Square.

MORTON, William Henry, age 48 of 38 Carlisle Street. Husband of Ethel L Morton. December 12, 1940, at 38 Carlisle Street.

MOSLEY, Joseph Edward, age 46; of 113, Maltravers Crescent. Husband of Gladys Mosley. Injured December 12, 1940, at 113, Maltravers Crescent; died December 12, 1940, at City General Hospital.

MOTTRAM, Blanche, aged 42; of 123, Musgrave Crescent. Wife of James Arthur Mottram. December 12, 1940, at 123, Musgrave Crescent.

MOTTRAM, James Arthur, age 46; MM and Bar; of 123, Musgrave Crescent. Husband of Blanche Mottram. December 12, 1940, at 123, Musgrave Crescent.

MOXON, Rowland, age 57; of 68, Grove Street, Pitsmoor. Husband of Mary Jane Moxon. December 13, 1940, at Grove Street.

MUNKS, Frank Hides, age 52; Constable Police War Reserve. Husband of Marjorie E Munks, of 36, Rockley Road. December 13, 1940, at Parkwood Road, Neepsend.

MURPHY, Arnold Arthur, age 19; of 66, Grove Street, Pitsmoor. Son of Kate and of the late William Hart Murphy. December 13, 1940, at 66, Grove Street.

MURPHY, Kate, age 61, of 66, Grove Street, Pitsmoor. Daughter of the late John and Alice Redfern, of 12, Attwood Street, Kidsgrove; widow of William Hart Murphy. December 13, 1940, at 66 Grove Street.

NAYLOR, Albert, age 35; of 17, Exeter Street. Husband of Elsie Naylor. December 12, 1940, at 17, Exeter Street.

NAYLOR, Elsie, age 36; of 17, Exeter Street. Daughter of John Henry and Florence Ann Stork; wife of Albert Naylor. December 12, 1940, at 17, Exeter Street.

NEALE, Anthony, age 16 months; of 119, Rock Street, Pitsmoor. Son of Ernest Corbett Neale and Edna Neale. December 13, 1940, at 119, Rock Street.

NEALE, Edna, age 23; of 119, Rock Street, Pitsmoor. Wife of Ernest Corbett Neale, December 13, 1940, at 119, Rock Street.

NEALE, Ernest Corbett, age 26, of 119, Rock Street, Pitsmoor. Son of Dorothy Agnes Davy (formerly Neale), of 9, Kilton Lane; husband of Edna Neale. December 13, 1940, at 119, Rock Street.

NEEDHAM, Charlotte, age 55; of 34, Greenhill Main Road. Wife of James Herbert Needham.

December 13, 1940, at 34, Greenhill Main Road.

NEEDHAM, Dorothy, age 14; of 34, Greenhill Main Road. Daughter of James Herbert and Charlotte Needham. December 13, 1940, at 34, Greenhill Main Road.

NEEDHAM, George Henry, age 49; ARP. Auxiliary Reserve. Husband of Bertha Needham of 58, Berners Road. December 13, 1940, at Clyde Works Shelter, Wicker.

NEEDHAM, James Herbert, age 48; of 34, Greenhill Main Road. Husband of Charlotte Needham. December 13, 1940, at 34, Greenhill Main Road.

NEWTON, Jessie, age 32; of 109, Pitsmoor Road. Daughter of Maud, and of the late James Newton. December 12, 1940, at 109, Pitsmoor Road.

NEWTON, Lily, age 44; of 109, Pitsmoor Road. Daughter of Maud, and of the late James Newton. December 12, 1940, at 109, Pitsmoor Road.

NEWTON, Mary, age 25; of 109, Pitsmoor Road. Daughter of Maud, and of the late James Newton. December 12, 1940, at 109, Pitsmoor Road.

NEWTON, Maud, age 64; of 109, Pitsmoor Road. Widow of James Newton. December 12, 1940, at 109, Pitsmoor Road.

NICHOLSON, Eva Emily, age 77; of 29, Wostenholme Road. December 13, 1940, at 29, Wostenholm Road.

NORMAN, Beatrice Hannah, age 33; of 11, Northcote Avenue. Daughter of Mr and Mrs J A Curley, of 55, Penns Road, Heeley; wife of Bernard Samuel Norman. December 13, 1940, at 11, Northcote Avenue.

NUTTALL , Sarah Ann, age 58; of 168, Shoreham Street. Wife of Tom Nuttall. December 13, 1940, at 168, Shoreham Street.

NUTTALL Tom, age 58, of 168 Shoreham Street, husband of Sarah Ann Nuttall. December 13 1940, at 168 Shoreham Street.

OLDFIELD Ernest, age 37, husband of Mary Marjorie Oldfield of 409 Mapperley Plains, Nottingham. December 13 1940, at William Deacon's Bank, The Moor.

OLDFIELD Jennie, age 41, of 41 Cookswood Road, daughter of Sam and Jane Oldfield of 86 Molton Street. December 12 1940, at Nottingham Cliff.

OLDFIELD Michael Brian, age 6, of 39 Broomhall Street. Step-son of Robert Wild. December 12 1940, at 39 Broomhall Street.

OLNEY Arthur, age 50, of Church Army Hostel, Campo Lane, son of Jessie Olney of South Yorkshire Hospital, December 12 1940, at Church Army Hostel.

PALMER Beatrice, age 22, of 39 Hawksley Avenue, daughter of Mr and Mrs Chapman of 32 Adkins Road; wife of Norman Mons Palmer. December 13 1940, at 39 Hawksley Avenue.

PALMER Gertrude, age 56, of 39 Hawksley Avenue, wife of S Palmer. December 13 1940, at 39 Hawksley Avenue.

PALMER Norman Mons, age 26, of Hawksley Avenue, son of S Palmer and of Gertrude Palmer; husband of Beatrice Palmer. December 13 1940, at 39 Hawksley Avenue.

PARAMORE Thomas, age 35, FAP member, son of Anne Paramore, of 267 Ringinglow Road, husband of Lilian Paramore, of the same address. December 12 1940, at Westbrook Bank.

PARDON Joseph, age 40, fireman, NFS. Son of Joseph and Florence Pardon, of 12 Lister Crescent, Gleadless; husband of Mary Pardon, of 4 Lister Crescent. Injured April 25 1944, at Prince of Wales Road; died April 26 1944, at Royal Hospital.

PARKER Annie, age 62, of 36 Barrack Lane, daughter of Mr and Mrs Trigg, of 26 Industry Street, Walkley; widow of John Parker. December 12 1940, at 36 Barrack Lane.

PARKIN Annie Amelia, age 64, of 16 Fleet Street, widow of T Parkin. December 15 1940, at 16 Fleet Street.

PARKIN Florence, age 25, of 16 Fleet Street, daughter of Annie Amelia, and of the late T Parkin. December 15 1940, 16 Fleet St.

PARKIN Maurice, age 42, husband of Florence A Parkin, of 107 Sellars Street. December 13 1940, at Porter Street shelter.

PARKINSON Harold F, age 42, fireman, NFS, husband of Isobel H Parkinson of 161 Folds Lane. Injured December 29 1942; died August 11 1943 at Sheffield.

PEACE Ernest, age 33, son of Dan Peace of 106 Clay Pit Lane, Rawmarsh, Rotherham; husband of Nellie Peace, of 47 Rush Avenue, Rawmarsh. December 12 1940, at Marples Hotel, Fitzalan Square.

PEACE Ezra, age 49, son of Dan Peace, of 106 Clay Pit Lane, Rawmarsh, Rotherham; husband of Alice Peace, of 313 Sheffield Road. December 12 1940, at Marples Hotel, Fitzalan Square.

PEAKER George Frederick, age 41, son of Mary A and George Andrew Peaker, of 28 Manor Oaks Place, Wybourn Estate; husband of Emily Peaker of 4 Keppel Road, Low Shiregreen. December 12 1940, at Haymarket.

PLACE Rosetta, age 31, of 30 Cockayne Place, Meersbrook, wife of Sydney Place. December 13 1940, at 30 Cockayne Place.

PEARSON Gertrude, age 66, of 163 Machon Bank Road, wife of William Henry Pearson. December 12 1940, at 163 Machon Bank Road.

PEARSON Phoebe, age 78, of 505 Queens Road. December 15 1940, at Bolsover Road.

PEARSON Rita Joan, age 19, of 163 Machon Bank Road, daughter of William Henry and Gertrude Pearson. December 12 1940, at 163 Machon Bank Road.

PEARSON William Henry, age 69, of 163 Machon Bank Road, husband of Gertrude Pearson. December 12 1940, at 163 Machon Bank Road.

PETTY Annie, age 24, of 22 Fleet Street, Brightside, daughter of Mary (Polly) Hurt; wife of James Petty. December 15 1940, at 22 Fleet Street.

PETTY James, age 31, of 22 Fleet Street, Brightside, husband of Annie Petty. Injured December 15 1940, at 22 Fleet Street, died December 17 1940. General Hospital.

PETTY Raymond, age 22 months, of 22 Fleet Street, Brightside, son of James and Annie Petty. December 15 1940, 22 Fleet St.

PICKERING Albert, age 67, of 76 Montgomery Road, Nether Edge, husband of Sarah Pickering. December 12 1940, at 76 Montgomery Road.

PICKERING Sarah, age 68, of 76 Montgomery Road, Nether Edge, wife of Albert Pickering. December 12 1940, at 76 Montgomery Road.

PINDER Arthur, age 25, of 14 Perigree Road, son of Fred and Jenny Pinder, of 170 Cartmell Road; husband of Kathleen May Pinder. December 13 1940, at 16 Perigree Road.

PINDER, Kathleen May, age 23; WVS; of 14, Perigree Road. Wife of Arthur Pinder. December 13, 1940, at 16, Perigree Road.

POYNTER, Ada, age 50; of 103, Pitsmoor Road. Wife of Wallace Poynter. December 12, 1940, at 103, Pitsmoor Road.

PRINCE, George William Leonard, age 57. Son of George and Minnie Prince, of Arbourthorne Road; husband of Florence Prince, of 116, Wordsworth Avenue, Parson Cross. December 12, 1940, at Hermitage Inn, London Road.

PUGH William Isaac, age 70, of 9 St Mary's Road, husband of Florence Pugh. December 13 1940, at 9 St Mary's Road.

RACKHAM, Noreen, age 23; of 72, Broomhall Street. Wife of S Rackham. December 12, 1940, at Marples Hotel, Fitzalan Square.

RANDS, Claud, age 43, of 118, St Mary's Road. Husband of Margaret Rands. December 13, 1940, at 118, St Mary's Road.

RAWLINS, David, age 2 months; of 40, Joshua Road. Son of J Rawlins and of Doris Rawlins. December 12, 1940, at 40, Joshua Road.

RAWLINS, Doris, age 26; of 40, Joshua Road. Wife of J Rawlins. December 12, 1940, at 40, Joshua Road.

RAWNSLEY, Malcolm, age 41; Fireman, NFS; of 1, Dawlish Grove, Leeds. Husband of Gladys Annie Rawnsley. Injured November 28, 1944, Rockingham Street; died January 2, 1945, at Sheffield.

RAWSON, Florence, age 39; of 7, Thirza Street. Daughter of Mr and Mrs Samuel Hartley, of 198, Rushdale Road; wife of A Rawson. Injured December 12, 1940, at Thirza Street; died December 13, 1940, at Royal Infirmary.

RAYNES, Charles, age 35; Air Raid Warden; of 10, Hollythorpe Crescent. Husband of Constance Raynes. December 12, 1940, at Bramall Lane.

RAYNES, Constance, age 36; Air Raid Warden; of 10, Hollythorpe Crescent. Wife of Charles Raynes. December 12, 1940, at Bramall Lane.

RAYNOR, Henry Vincent, age 47. Husband of Claudine Raynor, of 301, Sheffield Road, Tinsley. December 12, at Marples Hotel, Fitzalan Square.

REDFERN, Anthony William, age 2; of 43, Southey Hill, Parson Cross. Son of Hilda Redfern. March 14, 1941 43, Southey Hill.

REDFERN, Ellen, age 43; of 43, Southey Hill, Parson Cross. Daughter of Fred Griffin, of 57, Cookson Road; wife of William Refern. March 14, 1941, at 43, Southey Hill.

REDFERN, Joyce, age 15; of 43, Southey Hill, Parson Cross. Daughter of William and Ellen Redfern.

REDFERN, Kathleen, age 20; of 43, Southey Hill, Parson Cross. Daughter of William and Ellen Redfern. March 14, 1941, at 43, Southey Hill.

REDFERN, William, age 42; of 43, Southey Hill, Parson Cross. Son of Thomas Redfern, of 272, Fox Hill Road, Wadsley Bridge; husband of Ellen Redfern. March 14, 1941, at 43, Southey Hill.

RHODES, Maurice, age 32, of 358, Gleadless Road, Heeley. Son of Thomas and Eliza Rhodes, of 37, Boyton Street, Heeley; husband of Beatrice Annie Rhodes. Injured December 12, 1940, at 358, Gleadless Road; died December 13, 1940, at Royal Hospital Annexe, Fulwood.

RICHARDS, Eli, age 60; of 42, Joshua Road, Nether Edge. Son of the late Mr and Mrs Richards, of Flintshire, North Wales; husband of Lily Catherine Richards. December 12, 1940, at 42, Joshua Road.

RICHARDS, Lily Catherine, age 59; of 42, Joshua Road, Nether Edge. Daughter of the late Mr and Mrs Hill, of Flintshire, North Wales; wife of Eli Richards. December 12, 1940, at 42, Joshua Road.

RICHARDSON, Harold, age 17. Son of G and T Richardson, of 170, Maltravers Road, Wybourn Estate. Injured December 12, 1940, at 170, Maltravers Road; died December 13, 1940, at Children's Hospital.

RILEY, Dinah Chantry, age 24; of 3, Court, 1, House, Bangor Street. Daughter of Harry and Clara Emily Bower; wife of Arthur Riley. December 13, 1940, at 3, Court, 1, House, Bangor Street.

RILEY, Michael, age 6; of 3, Court, 1, House, Bangor Street. Son of Arthur Riley, and of Dinah Chantry Riley. December 13, 1940, at 3, Court, 1, House, Bangor Street.

RILEY, Peter, age 17 months; of 3, Court, 1, House, Bangor Street. Son of Arthur Riley, and of Dinah Chantry Riley. December 13, 1940, at 3, Court, 1, House, Bangor Street.

ROBERTS, Elsie May, age 21. Daughter of Harry and Elsie May Roberts, of 680, Abbeydale Road. Decemgber 13, 1940, at Porter Street Shelter.

ROBERTS, John Henry, age 65; of 159, Eyre Street. December 12, 1940, at Nether Edge Hospital.

ROBINSON Leslie, age 30, of 44 Barrack Lane, husband of A Robinson. December 12 1940, at 44 Barrack Lane.

RODGERS Wilhelmena, age 76, of 40 Joshua Road, widow of H Rodgers. December 12 1940, at 40 Joshua Road.

ROE Bernard Douglas, age 22, of 18 Nether Green Road, son of Flora Roe. December 12 1940, at Marples Hotel, Fitzalan Square.

ROSE Henry, age 74, of 94 Bloor Street, husband of Eveline Rose. December 12 1940, at 94 Bloor Street.

SANDERS Ethel, age 40, of 97 Valley Road, wife of George Frederick Sanders. December 12 1940, at 97 Valley Road.

SALISBURY, Victor George Thomas, age 42; Air Raid Warden. Husband of Florence May Salisbury, of 300, Greenland Road, Darnall. December 15, 1940, at ARP post, Coleford Road.

SANDERS, George Frederick, age 43; of 97, Valley Road. Husband of Ethel Saunders. 12 December, 1940, at 97 Valley Road.

SANDS, William, age 33; of 26, Wallace Road. Husband of L Sands. December 13, 1940, at Royal Infirmary.

SANSOM, Harry, age 32. Husband of Nellie Sansom, of 5, Wilmot Terrace, Owlerton. December 12, 1940, at Marples Hotel, Fitzalan Square.

SAVILLE, Jane, age 45. Wife of A S Saville, of 39, Uttley Street. December 15, 1940, at 30 Uttley Street.

SHAW, John William, age 29; Air Raid Warden; Fire Fighter. Son of Mr H Shaw, of 60, Leader Road, Hillsborough; husband of Marjorie Shaw, of Top House. Mawson Lane, Worrall. December 13, 1940, at Sheaf Street.

SHEARSTONE, Herbert Eric, age 23; of 29, Brushfield Grove, Frecheville. December 12, 1940, of 38, Joshua Road.

SHEPHARD, Walter, age 72; Air Raid Warden; of 6, Machon Bank, Nether Edge. December 13, 1940, at Abbeydale Road.

SHERWOOD, George Parker, age 60; of 19, Carfield Avenue. Husband of Lilian C Sherwood. December 12, 1940, at 19 Carfield Avenue .

SHOOTER, Lilian, age 32. Daughter of James and Emma Dodd, of 152, Cross Lane, Crookes; wife of Albert Shooter, of 4, Dawlands Close, Manor Estate. December 12, 1940, at Marples Hotel, Fitzalan Square.

SIDDALL, Elsie, age 45; of 144, Sutherland Road. Wife of G Siddall. December 12, 1940, at Marples Hotel, Fitzalan Square.

SILVESTER, Ethel, age 50; of 72, Nether Edge Road. Wife of Fred Silvester. December 12, 1940, at 74, Nether Edge Road.

SILVESTER, Fred, age 51; Home Guard; of 72, Nether Edge Road. Husband of Ethel Silvester. December 12, 1940, at 74, Nether Edge Road.

SIMMONITE, Henry, age 68; of 69, Whixley Road, Darnall. Husband of Edith Simmonite. December 15, 1940, at 69, Whixley Road.

SIMPSON, Elizabeth, 76; of 80, Burngreave Road. Widow of F Simpson. December 18, 1940, at 80, Burngreave Road.

SIMPSON, Margaret, age 23; of 27, Bressingham Road. Daughter of Mary Ellen, and of the late Samuel Simpson. December 13, 1940, at 25, Bressingham Road.

SIMPSON, Mary Ellen, age 58; of 27, Bressingham Road. Widow of Samuel Simposn. December 13, 1940, at 25, Bressingham Road.

SINGLETON, Emma, age 77; of 32, Crookes Road. Widow of J Singleton. December 12, 1940, at 32, Crookes Road.

SKINNER, Elizabeth, age 45. Wife of T R Skinner, of 17, Park Street, Worksop, Nottinghamshire. December 12, 1940, at 116, Shirebrook Road.

SLACK, Alice Gertrude, age 67; of 51, Croft Buildings, Campo Lane. Daughter of the late Joseph and Kate Slack. December 12, 1940, at 51, Croft Buildings.

SLACK, Phyllis May, age 30; of 58, St Mary's Road. Daughter of Agnes Maud, and of the late Thomas Leyland; wife of Alan Slack. December 13, 1940, at 34, St Mary's Road.

SLACK, Stanley, age 29; of 84, Hermitage Street. December 12, 1940, outside Empire Theatre.

SMITH, Albert, age 70; of 15, St Barnabas Road. December 12, 1940, at Nether Edge Hospital.

SMITH, Charles Frederick, age 51; of 4, Leppings Lane. Husband of Alethea Smith. December 12, 1940, at Marples Hotel, Fitzalan Square.

SMITH, Charlotte Emily, age 55; of 45, Kyle Crescent. Wife of Charles William Smith. Injured March 14, 1941, at 45, Kyle Crescent; died March 16, 1941, at City General Hospital.

SMITH, Helena (Lena), age 40, of 13, Exter Street. Wife of Thomas Launders Smith. December 12, 1940, at 13, Exter Street.

(for **SMITH,** Iris see WORTLEY list).

SMITH, Madge, age 24. Wife of Fred Smith, of 112, Basford Street, Darnall. December 11, 1940, at Marples Hotel, Fitzalan Square.

SMITH Percival Henry Goodacre, age 25, son of Percy R and Lily Smith, of 86 Danville Street, Pitsmoor. December 12 1940, at 65 Ellesmere Road.

SOUTH Samuel, age 69, Air Raid Warden, son of Samuel and Sarah South, of Burngreave Steet, husband of Frances Gertrude South, of 72 Psalter Lane. Injured September 1942, at Psalter Lane; died September 25 1944, at Nether Edge Hospital.

SPENCER Frederick Parkes, age 36, Police Fireman, Sheffield Borough Police, of 22 Chief Fire Station, Rockingham Street, son of Frederick Parkes Spencer, and Elsie Spencer, of 139 Bradway Road, Bradway; husband of Edna Spencer. December 12 1940, outside Empire Theatre.

SPOTSWOOD Walter, age 28, of 87 Maltravers Terrace, husband of Beatrice Spotswood. Injured December 12 1940, at 87 Maltravers Terrace; died December 13 1940, at Royal Hospital.

STACEY Tom, age 31, AFS, Fire Fighter, husband of Winifred Stacey, of 90 Paper Mill Road, Shiregreen Estate. December 12 1940, at corner of Castle Street and Castle Green.

STANTON Arthur, age 62, of The Lodging House, Trafalgar Street. December 13 1940, at William Deacon's Bank, The Moor.

STEEL Annie Elizabeth, age 66, of 12 Westbrook Bank, Sharrow, daughter of the late Richard and Elizabeth Howe; wife of George Thomas Steel. December 12 1940, at Westbrook Road.

STEEL Irene, age 26, daughter of the late Mr and Mrs Oxspring, wife of A Steel, of 341 Bellhouse Road. December 12 1940, at Marples Hotel, Fitzalan Square.

STEEL Olive, age 26, of 12 Westbrook Road, Sharrow, wife of Kenneth Steel. Injured December 12 1940, at 12 Westbrook Road; died December 13 1940, at Women's Hospital, Leavygreave Road.

STEVENS Robert, age 20, son of E and B Stevens, of 7 Guest Road, Hunters Bar. December 15 1940, at 77 Whixley Road.

STEVENSON Annie, age 56, of 7 St Mary's Road, wife of Thomas Ernest Stevenson. December 13 1940, at 7 St Mary's Road.

STEVENSON Thomas Ernest, age 54, of 7 St Mary's Road, husband of Annie Stevenson. Injured December 13 1940 at 7 St Mary's Road; died same day at Royal Hospital.

STORK Florence Ann, age 62, of 2 Exeter Street, wife of John Henry Stork. December 12 1940, at 17 Exeter Street.

STORK John Henry, age 73, of 2 Exeter Steet, husband of Florence Ann Stork. December 12 1940, at 17 Exeter Street.

STRATFORD Charles, age 65, of 256 Crookes, husband of Mary Stratford. Injured December 12 1940, at Sheffield; died December 13 1940 at Royal Infirmary.

STRATTON Connie, age 28, daughter of Arthur Benjamin and Clara Stratton, of 30 Bartlett Road, Southey Green. Injured December 13 1940, at Porter Street shelter; died December 20 1940, at Royal Hospital.

SUMMERSGILL Herbert, age 60, Air Raid Warden, of 62 Glen Road, husband of Hannah Mary Summersgill. Injured December 13 1940, at Glen Road, died December 15 1940, at Royal Hospital Annexe, Fulwood.

SWABY John William, age 38, AFS, husband of Loiuisa Swaby, of 46 Boynton Road, Shirecliffe. December 13 1940, at Burgess Street.

SWANSTON Charles Arnold, age 25, son of Alexander and Ethel Swanston, of 69 Findon Street, Hillsborough; husband of Lilian Swanston of 13 Lofthouse Road. December 13 1940 at Ibbotson's Works, Alma Street.

SWIFT Elsie, age 31, of 20 Daffodil Road, Shiregreen, wife of George Robert Swift (HM Forces). December 13 1940, at 20 Daffodil Road.

TAFF William, age two, son of William and Clara Taff, of 40 Cattal Street, Darnall. December 12 1940, at 3 Fieldhead Road.

TALBOT Frank, age 38, of 108 Hodgson Street, son of E Talbot of 22 Lindsay Avenue; husband of Nellie Talbot. Injured December 12 1940, at Sheffield; died December 14 1940 at Royal Infirmary.

TAYLOR Arthur Colin, age 49, of 165 Machon Bank Road, son of Arthur James and Ellen Taylor. December 12 1940, at 165 Machon Bank Road.

TAYLOR Edgar, age 41, of 118 St Mary's Road, son of Mr and Mrs F Taylor of 30 Victoria Street, Brampton, Chesterfield. December 13 1940, at 118 St Mary's Road.

TAYLOR George Herbert, age 42, of 341 Chesterfield Road, son of B Taylor of 36 Ellerton Road, Firth Park, and of the late Herbert Taylor; husband of Elsie Taylor. December 12 1940, at Marples Hotel, Fitzalan Square.

TAYLOR James Hedley, age 77, of 9 Ellesmere Road, husband of Mabel Taylor. Injured December 12 1940, at 9 Ellesmere Road, died December 14, 1940, at City General Hospital.

TAYLOR, Lily, age 46. Daughter of Annie Taylor of 45, Holme Lane, Hillsborough. December 12, 1940, at Marples Hotel, Fitzalan Square.

TAYLOR, Percy Sorby, age 53; of 165, Machon Bank Road. Son of Arthur James and Ellen Taylor. December 12, 1940, at 165, Machon Bank Road.

TEMPEST, Derek, age 4; of 287, Ellesmere Road, Pitsmoor. Son of James Hilton Tempest, and Gladys Eveline Tempest. October 12, 1941, at 287, Ellesmere Road.

TEMPEST, Edna, age 17; of 287, Ellesmere Road, Pitsmoor. Daughter of James Hilton Tempest and Gladys Eveline Tempest. Injured October 12, 1941, at 287, Ellesmere Road; died October 13, 1941, at City General Hospital.

TEMPEST, Gladys Eveline, age 43; of 287, Ellesmere Road, Pitsmoor. Daughter of Hebdon Flower Lancaster, of 8, Woodlands Grove, Stanningley, Leeds, and of the late Rose Anne Lancaster; wife of James Hilton Tempest. October 12, 1941, at 287, Ellesmere Road.

TEMPEST, James Hilton, age 41; of 287, Ellesmere Road, Pitsmoor. Son of Jane Tempest, of 179, Highfield Cottages, Fartown, Pudsey, and of the late Arthur Tempest; husband of Gladys Eveline Tempest. October 12, 1941, at 287, Ellesmere Road.

THEAKER, Sam Clifford, aged 52; of 74, Summerfield Street. Son of Samuel Theaker, of 9, Rippon Road. Injured May 9, 1941, at Summerfield Street; died same day at Royal Hospital.

THOMPSON, Alice, age 50; of 10, West Don Street. Wife of Fred Thompson. December 13, 1940, at 23, West Don Street.

THOMPSON, Fred, age 50; of 10, West Don Street. Husband of Alice Thompson. December 13, 1940, at 12, West Don Street.

THOMPSON, Fred, age 26; of 33, Oakland Road. December 13, 1940, at 12, West Don Street.

THOMPSON, Kathleen, age 26. Wife of E Thompson, of 33, Oakland Road. December 12, 1940, at 12, West Don Street.

THORPE, Gertrude, age 27. Daughter of Mr and Mrs W. Bacon of Back 317, Abbeydale Road; wife of AB James Alfred Thorpe, RN. December 12, 1940, at Marples Hotel, Fitzalan Square.

THURTLE, John Henry, age 60; of 119 Rock Street, Pitsmoor. Son of the late M Thurtle; husband of the late Grace Thurtle. December 13, 1940, at 119, Rock Street.

TINGLE, Kate, age 74; of 98, Cobden View Road. Widow of H Tingle. December 13, 1940, at 98, Cobden View Road.

TINKER, Francis Ernest, age 54; of 159, Rock Street, Pitsmoor. Son of Francis A and Hannah Tinker, of 43, Firth Park Road. December 12, 1940, at 159, Rock Street.

TOOKEY, Rose, age 45; of 35, Sheaf Gardens. Widow of David Tookey. December 13, 1940, at 118, St Mary's Road.

TORR, George Edward, age 39; Air Raid Warden. Husband of Edith Torr, of 85, Clough Bank, Masbrough, Rotherham. Injured September 26, 1940, at W F Flather Ltd, Standard Steel Works, Sheffield Road; died September 28, 1940, at Royal Infirmary.

TRAVERS, William, age 51. Husband of Annnie Travers, of 29, Normandale Road. December 12, 1940, at Marples Hotel, Fitzalan Square.

TUCKWOOD, Horace, age 31; of 112, Wulfric Road. December 12, 1940, at Samuel Osborne Cylde Works Shelter, Wicker.

TURNER, Arthur Gilbert, age 22; of 116, Shirebrook Road, Heeley. Son of Frank Turner, of 25, Harwood Street, Highfield, and of the late Mary Turner; husband of Mary Agatha Turner. December 12, 1940, at 116, Shirebrook Road.

TURNER, Harold, age 35; of 39, Southey Hill. March 14, 1941, at 37, Southey Hill.

TURNER, Mary Agatha, age 21; of 116, Shirebrook Road, Heeley. Daughter of James A. and Bertha McIntyre, of 73, Gregory Road; wife of Arthur Gilbert Turner. December 12, 1940, at 116, Shirebrook Road.

TURNER, Sarah Ellen, aged 74; of 3, Fieldhead Road. December 12, 1940, at 3, Fieldhead Road.

TURTON, Margaret Jane, age 71; of 116, Shirebrook Road. Widow of Thurston George Turton. December 12, 1940, at 116, Shirebrook Road.

VERNON, Clara, age 38. Wife of Thomas Vernon, of 9, The Greenway, Meadow Head. December 12, 1940, at 116, Shirebrook Road.

VERNON, Minnie, age 50. Daughter of the late David Vernon. December 12, 1940, at 111, Pitsmoor Road.

VERNON, Stanley Hadfield, age 17. Son of Thomas Vernon, of 9,

The Greenway, Meadow Head, and of Clara Vernon. Injured December 14, 1940, at 34, Myrtle Road; died same day at City General Hospital.

WALKER, Alfreda Elizabeth, age 11; of 6, Cricket Inn Road. Daughter of Isaac Walker. December 13, 1940, at Arbourthorne School.

WALKER, William Henry, age 29. Son of Ada Walker, of 182, Penistone Road. December 12, 1940, at Marples Hotel, Fitzalan Square.

WALLACE, Albert, age 30; AFS. Son of Florence Wallace, of 39, Fawley Road. December 12, 1940, at Marples Hotel, Fitzalan Square.

WALLACE, William, age 74; of 356, Gleadless Road. December 12, 1940, at 356, Gleadless Road.

WARHURST, Samuel Frank, age 56; of 11, Daffdil Road, Shiregreen. Son of the late Mr and Mrs Warhurst, of Corby Street. December 13, 1940, at 11, Daffodil Road.

WESLEY, Maud, age 37. Daughter of Linley, and of the late Maud Worth; wife of Maurice Wesley, of 233, West Green Road, Tottenham, Middlesex. Injured December 12, 1940, at 146, Steade Road; died same day at Royal Hospital.

WEST, Dennis, age 11; of 7, Windsor Road, Meersbrook. Son of G B West, and of Elsie West. December 13, 1940, at 7, Windsor Road.

WEST, Edna, age 34; of 95, Rock Street, Pitsmoor. Wife of Herbert West. December 13, 1940, at 95, Rock Street.

WEST, Elizabeth, age 63; of 95, Rock Street, Pitsmoor. Wife of Harry West. December 13, 1940, at 95, Rock Street.

WEST, Elsie, age 35; of 7, Windsor Road, Meersbrook. Daughter of Mr and Mrs A Whitaker, of 27, Carter Place, Heeley; wife of G B West. December 13, 1940, at 7, Windsor Road.

WEST, Geoffrey, age 4; of 95, Rock Street, Pitsmoor. Son of Herbert West, and of Edna West. December 13, 1940, at 95, Rock Street.

WEST, Harry, age 67; of 95, Rock Street, Pitsmoor. Husband of Elizabeth West. December 13, 1940, at 95, Rock Street.

WESTBY, Eva, age 34. Wife of Richard Westby, of 30, Southey Drive. December 12, 1940, at Marples Hotel, Fitzalan Square.

WILD, George, age 43; of 94, Kyle Crescent, Parson Cross. Son of Mr and Mrs G Wild. March 14, 1941, at 94, Kyle Crescent.

WILD, Patricia May, age 22, months; of 39, Broomhall Street. Daughter of Robert Wild. December 12, 1940, at 39, Broomhall Street.

WILD, Robert, age 43; of 39, Broomhall Street. December 12, 1940, at 39, Broomhall Street.

WILDE, William Trevor, age 23; B.Sc., Ph.D.; Gas Identification Service. Son of Mrs E M Wilde, of 67, Marsh House Road. October 20, 1941, Clarkehouse Road.

WILDSMITH, Elizabeth, age 38. Daughter of Mary Wolstenholme, of 2, Court, 1, Fulton Road, Walkley; widow of S Wildsmith. December 12, 1940, at Marples Hotel, Fitzalan Square.

WILSON, Edith Grace, age 30. Daughter of Mr and Mrs Henry Summer, of Gothic Cottage, Peascod Street, Windsor, Berkshire; wife of Thomas Wilson, of 5, Bastock Road. December 12, 1940, at Marples Hotel, Fitzalan Square.

WILSON, Thomas, age 52; A.R.P. Ambulance Driver; of 86, Ecclesall Road. December 12, 1940, at Westbrook Bank.

WINSLADE, Edna, age 15; of 9, Finlay Street. Daughter of William and Edith Alice Winslade. Injured at 1, Court, 2, Finlay Street; died August 29, 1940, at Royal Infirmary.

WINTER, Frank Donald, age 40; Air Raid Warden. Husband of Lilian Winter, of 110, Coleford Road. Injured December 15, 1940, at A.R.P. post, Coleford Road; died December 16, 1940, at City General Hospital.

WOOD, Percy, age 44; B.R.C.S. Ambulance Service. Husband of Florence May Wood, of 12, Thorpe House Avenue, Norton Lees. December 13, 1940, at Shoreham Street.

WOODCOCK, Winifred, age 16; of 245, Hanover Street. Daughter of Mr and Mrs A. Woodcock. December 12, 1940, at 245, Hanover Street.

WOODLIFF, Bob, age 55; of 12, Daffodil Road, Shiregreen. Son of the late John and Harriet Woodliff. Injured December 13, 1940, at 12, Daffodil Road; died December 14, 1940, at City General Hospital.

WOODS, Betty, age 21; of 38, Joshua Road. Step-daughter of Mr J Fox. December 12, 1940, at 38, Joshua Road.

WOOLLEN, Ethel, age 46; of 133, Crookesmoor Road. Wife of Vernon Brookes Woollen. December 13, 1940, at 133, Crookesmoor Road.

WOOLLEN, Vernon Brookes, age 48; of 133, Crookesmoor Road. Son of Mr and Mrs J J Woollen, of 23, Springwood Road, Heeley; husband of Ethel Woollen. December 13, 1940, at 133, Crookesmoor Road.

WORTH, Linley, age 64; of 146, Steade Road. Husband of the late Maud Worth. December 12, 1940, at 146, Steade Road.

WOLSTENHOLME, Dorothy, age 18; of 38, St Mary's Road.

Daughter of Harold and Olive Wolstenholme. December 13, 1940, at 38, St Mary's Road.

WOLSTENHOLME, Harold, age 46, of 38, St Mary's Road. Husband of Olive Wolstenholme. December 13, 1940, at 38, St Mary's Road.

WOLSTENHOLME, Hazel, age 18 months, of 38, St Mary's Road. Daughter of Harold and Olive Wolstenholme. December 13, 1940, at 38, St Mary's Road.

WOLSTENHOLME, Peter, age 2; of 38, St Mary's Road. Son of Harold and Olive Wolstenholme. December 13, 1940, at 38, St Mary's Road.

WOLSTENHOLME, Norman, age 12, of 38, St Mary's Road. Son of Harold and Olive Wolstenholme. December 13, 1940, at 38, St Mary's Road.

WOLSTENHOLME, Olive, age 42; of 38, St Mary's Road. Wife of Harold Wolstenholme. December 13, 1940, at 38, St Mary's Road.

WOLSTENHOLME, Ann Eliza, age 73; of 66, Thirlwell Road. Widow of Francis Farshaw Wolstenholme. December 12, 1940, at 66, Thirlwell Road.

WOLSTENHOLME, John Charles, age 39; Home Guard; of 66, Thirlwell Road. Son of Ann Eliza, and of the late Francis Farshaw Wolstenholme. December 12, 1940, at 66, Thirlwell Road.

WOLSTENHOLME, Vera Kathleen age 20; of 66, Thirlwell Road. Daughter of Francis Donald and Gladys Wolstenholme, December 12, 1940, at 66, Thirlwell Road.

WOLSTENHOLME, Florence Elizabeth, age 30, FAP member; of 25, Endowood Road, Millhouses. Daughter of William and Florence Rutter, of 5, Forth Street, Leeman Road, York; wife of Alan Wolstenholme, December 12, 1940, at 25, Endowood Road.

WRIGHT, Florence, age 75; of 97, Bloor Street. Widow of S. Wright. December 13, 1940, at Royal Infirmary.

WRIGHT, Harry, age 59; A.R.P. Rescue Service; of 122, Stannington View Road. December 12, 1940, at Westbrook Bank.

YANCE, Edith Mary, age 65; of 176, Devonshire Street. Daughter of the late David and Sarah Ann Avison, of Scarborough; widow of William Yance. December 12, 1940, at 176, Devonshire Street.

A final word

The Blitz tore the heart out of Sheffield but put heart into its people. They had been enjoying a false state of security right up to December 12, 1940, insisting on living as normal as was possible in those abnormal times. But the two Blitz attacks brought home to Sheffield the realities of war.

There were acts of tremendous heroism carried out by people who would never have dreamed of themselves as heroes. Maybe that is the secret of Sheffield's survival through those dark days. The reaction to extraordinary situations was to behave in as ordinary a way as possible. And if that meant bringing out the best in your personality and character, then Sheffield could only become the wealthier for it. It certainly helped the people of Sheffield face up to the rest of the war. There were several more raids. Granted, none of them were as destructive as those of December 12 and 15, 1940, but they were severe enough. Eight people died and another 55 were injured when bombs and land mines were dropped on Wadsley and Southey areas, leaving 400 people homeless. Another eight died and 19 were injured in October of 1941 during a raid on Ellesmere Road, Scott Road and Grimesthorpe Road, in which many houses were demolished or severely damaged. In May, high explosives and incendiaries were dropped on Heeley, Abbeydale, Millhouses and Sharrow, killing two people and harming another 36. And a single bomb was dropped by a lone raider in February, 1941, killing a woman and injuring five other people. The feeling all along was that the steelworks were Hitler's prime target, as indeed they were. But if that is the only thing the Germans were intent on destroying then it is difficult to reconcile their continued attacks where the civilian population bore the brunt of their ferocity. It is not beyond imagination for the German High Command to have decreed the people of Sheffield a legitimate target. After all, without them, the steelworks would have ground to a halt and to terrorise them may have had an effect on the production of Britain's weapons of war. However, in the same way that the intention to bomb the steelworks into silence had been a failure, if the intention was also to blast the people of Sheffield into submission, this too came to nothing. They worked on throughout the war, keeping the steel and engineering works operating round the clock and the front line troops supplied with the tools they needed for their bloody but necessary work.

Sadly, 60 years on, the steelworks have all but gone. The drop hammer beat from the heart of the industrial quarter is muffled today. What Hitler failed to do, market forces have achieved. Yet that spirit which saw Sheffield through the Blitz lives on in a northern character which has a tendency to shrug its shoulders at adversity and get on with life.

Today, the children, grandchildren and great grandchildren of the survivors of those who experienced the Blitz are shrugging their shoulders and getting on with their lives.